CAMBRIDGE INTRODUCTION TO THE HISTORY OF MANKIND · TOPIC BOOK
GENERAL EDITOR · TREVOR CAIRNS

European Soldiers 1550-1650

Geoffrey and Angela Parker

CAMBRIDGE UNIVERSITY PRESS
Cambridge
London · New York · Melbourne

Maps and diagrams by
Reg Piggott and Peter North

For Susanna and Edmund

Published by the Syndics of the Cambridge University Press
The Pitt Building, Trumpington Street, Cambridge CB2 1RP
Bentley House, 200 Euston Road, London NW1 2DB
32 East 57th Street, New York, NY 10022, USA
296 Beaconsfield Parade, Middle Park, Melbourne 3206, Australia

© Cambridge University Press 1977

First published 1977

Printed in Great Britain at
the Alden Press, Oxford

Library of Congress cataloguing in publication data
Parker, Geoffrey, 1943–

European soldiers, 1550–1650.

(Cambridge introduction to the history of mankind)

SUMMARY: Discusses the life of a European soldier in the
late sixteenth and early seventeenth centuries, including his training,
weapons, and conditions of service.

1. Soldiers – Europe – History – Juv. lit. 2. Armies – History –
Juv. lit. 3. Europe – History, Military – Juv. lit. 4. Nördlingen,
Battle of, 1634 – Juv. lit. [1. Soldiers – Europe – History. 2.
Armies – History. 3. Europe – History, Military. 4. Nördlingen,
Battle of, 1634]

I. Parker, Angela, joint author. 1943–   II. Title.
U765.P37   355.1'2'094   76-23423
ISBN 0 521 21020 8

Illustrations

The authors and publisher wish to thank the following individuals
and institutions for permission to reproduce illustrations.

Cover picture: Painting by Sebastian Vrancx, 'Attack on a Convoy',
1616. Reproduced by gracious permission of Her Majesty the
Queen.

p.4: Another painting of an ambush by Vrancx. Bayerisches
Nationalmuseum, Munich.

pp.6 and 7: The siege-works of Amiens in 1597 and today. From
Antiquity 150, June 1964. By permission of M. Roger Agache
and the editor.

p.8: Title page from John Cruso, *Militarie Instructions for the
Cavall'rie*, Cambridge 1632. Photograph by Cambridge University
Library.

p.9: Cannon-balls and bullets. By permission of Colin Martin,
Institute of Maritime Archaeology, University of St Andrews,
Scotland.

p.10: English letter, from Cheshire County Record Office, *Quarter
Sessions of 1660*, file 4, folio 64. (With thanks to Dr J. S. Morrill.)
Spanish letter, from Archivo General de Simancas, Spain, *Estado*,
legajo 608, folio 32.

p.11: Helmets from the Wallace Collection, London. Crown copyright.

pp.12 and 13: Three prints from Jacob de Gheyn, *The Use of
Weapons: Arquebus, Musket and Pike*, The Hague, 1607. Photographs by Cambridge University Library.

p.13 (right): Print from Jan Boxel, *A Picture of Arms Drill*, 3 vols.,
The Hague, 1673. Photographs by British Library.

p.14: Two Dutch prints. Left, by H. Goltzius, 1587; right, by
Hogenburg, 'The Siege of Wedde', 1593. Rijksprentenkabinet,
Rijksmuseum, Amsterdam.

p.15: Lance meets pike, from Johan Jakob von Wallhausen, *Military
Prowess on Horseback*, Frankfurt, 1616. Photograph by Cambridge University Library.

p.16: Two more drills by Wallhausen, these from *Military Prowess
on Foot*, Frankfurt, 1616. Photographs by Cambridge University
Library.

p.17: Swiss arms and armour. Schweizerisches Landesmuseum,
Zurich.

p.18: Gun drawings from Dudley Pope, *Guns*, Weidenfeld & Nicolson, 1969. Musket photograph by Colin Martin.

p.19: Musketeer meets horseman, from Wallhausen, *Military Prowess on Horseback*. Photograph by Cambridge University Library.

p.20: Armour from the Wallace Collection, London. Crown copyright. Drawing of armour from the Victoria and Albert Museum, London.

p.21: Cavalry from Cruso, *Militarie Instructions for the Cavall'rie*. Photograph by Cambridge University Library.
'Lobster pot' from the Tower of London. Crown copyright.

p.22: Painting by Pieter Snaeyers, 'La Toma de Aire-sur-le-Lis', 1641. Museo del Prado, Madrid.

p.24: Enlistment. Above, from L. Fronsperger, *Of the Imperial Law of War*, 3 vols., Frankfurt, 1571–3. Below, from Jacques Callot, *The Miseries of War*, Paris, 1633. Photographs by British Library.

p.25: *King Henry IV*, Part II, Act II scene 2, from the folio edition in the University Library, St Andrew's, Scotland. (With thanks to Dr C. G. Cruickshank.)

p.27: Engraving of Henry VIII's encampment near Portsmouth. Mansell Collection.

p.28: Engraving of Henry VIII's encampment in France. Society of Antiquaries, London.

p.29: How to erect a camp, from Fronsperger, *Of the Imperial Law of War*. Photograph by British Library.

p.31: Paintings by David Vinckeboons, 1620s. Rijksmuseum, Amsterdam.

p.32: Articles from the *Vasa*, from the Statens Sjöhistoriskamuseum, Wasavarvet, Stockholm.
Bowl from the *Trinidad Valencera*, by permission of Colin Martin, Institute of Maritime Archaeology, University of St Andrews, Scotland.

p.33: Detail from Pieter Brueghel, 'The Triumph of Death', 1562. Museo del Prado, Madrid.

p.34: Army on the march, from the Cabinet des Estampes, Bibliothèque Nationale, Paris.

p.35: Engraving by Jacob de Gheyn. Rijksmuseum, Amsterdam.

p.36: Engraving by Robert Streeter in Joshua Sprigge, *Anglia Rediviva*, London, 1647 Photograph by British Library.

p.38: Diagram from Leonard Digges, *An Arithmeticall Militarie Treatise, named Stratioticos, compendiously teaching the science of numbers requisite for the profession of a soldiour*, London, 1579. Photograph by Cambridge University Library.

p.40: Sketch of Champlain, 1613. Photograph by R.B. Fleming, Weidenfeld & Nicolson Ltd.

p.41: Page from Don Bernardo de Vargas Machuca, *Warfare in the Indies*, Madrid, 1599. Biblioteca Nacional, Madrid.

p.42: Extract from Sir John Smythe, *Instructions, Observations and Orders Mylitarie*, London, 1595. Photograph by British Library.

p.43: Diagram by Jan Boxel, 1673. Photograph by British Library.

p.44: Engravings from Callot, *The Miseries of War*. Photographs by British Library.

p.46: Painting by Rubens, 'The Battle of Nördlingen'. Reproduced by gracious permission of Her Majesty the Queen.

p.48: Estebanillo Gonzalez, frontispiece to the first edition of *The Life and Deeds of Estebanillo Gonzalez*, Antwerp, 1646. Photograph by Bibliothèque Nationale, Paris.
Seventeenth-century satire, photograph by Geoffrey Parker.

p.49: Pitching camp, from Wallhausen, *Military Prowess on Foot*. Photograph by Cambridge University Library.

p.51: Engraving by Hans Holbein, 'Schweizer Schlacht', 1530–2. Kupferstichkabinett, Basel.
Maps based on V. Wedgwood, *The Thirty Years War*.

pp.52 and 53: Battle of Nördlingen from Bibliothèque Nationale, Paris.

p.54: Plundering soldiers from Fronsperger, *Of the Imperial Law of War*. Photograph by British Library.

p.57: Woodcut from Hans von Gersdorff, *Field Manual of Wound Surgery*, Strasbourg, 1517. Photograph by British Library.
Instruments from William Clowes, *A Prooved Practise for all Young Chirurgians*, London, 1591. Photograph by Cambridge University Library.

p.58: Woodcut from Gersdorff, *Field Manual of Wound Surgery*. Photograph by British Library.

p.59: Artificial limbs from the Wellcome Institute for the History of Medicine, London.

p.60: Woodcut from Gersdorff, *Field Manual of Wound Surgery*. Photograph by British Library.

p.61: German print of Haarlem. Bibliothèque Nationale, Paris.

p.62: Zwingli's helmet and sword. Schweizerisches Landesmuseum, Zurich.

p.63: Painting by Lucas van Hillegaert. Rijksmuseum, Amsterdam.

p.64: Paintings of grenadiers by David Morier, 1751. Reproduced by gracious permission of Her Majesty the Queen.

Contents

A detail of a painting by Sebastian Vrancx, an artist who lived in Antwerp in the 17th century. The same man painted the picture which appears on the cover of this book. Both pictures show a wagon train being ambushed by a party of soldiers. On the cover we can see women being searched to find if they are hiding money or jewels about their persons. Those who are trying to run away are being hunted down and shot — as are some of those who remain. The scene here is almost as blood-thirsty. The man in the bottom left-hand corner is being murdered in cold-blood under the eyes of the commanding officer of the attackers, while the victorious troops are sharing out the possessions of those they have killed.

Introduction: how to find out

If we want to know what soldiers look like and what they do today, either we go out and see them for ourselves, or else we look in books for pictures and descriptions. It is almost the same for soldiers in the past. In the first place we can go to a museum and see the uniforms, the armour and the weapons which were used at various times. (Your own local museum will probably have something worn or used by the soldiers of the sixteenth and seventeenth centuries.) Then we can look around for one of the many towns and villages which were defended in Renaissance times with walls or a castle. Some of these have survived almost intact.

The castles at Deal and Camber on the Kent coast in England, built by Henry VIII in the 1540s to stop an expected invasion from France, are still perfectly preserved. So are the massive town ramparts of Berwick-upon-Tweed, built in the later sixteenth century to keep the Scots at bay, and the great castle

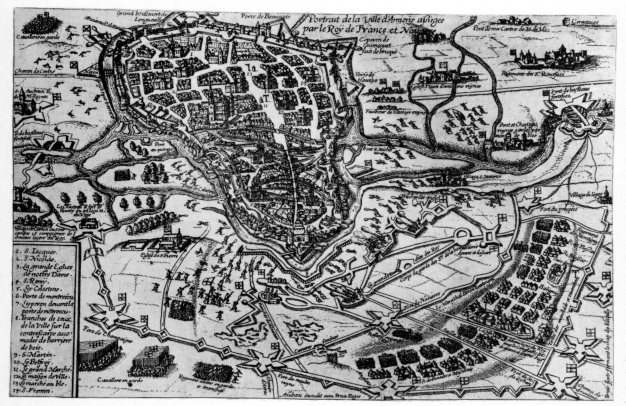

King Henry IV of France besieged the town of Amiens in northern France in 1597. It had been captured by the Spanish army. In this print which was made at the time you can see the earthwork ramparts built by Henry IV to shield his men from the guns of Amiens and from the risk of attack by a Spanish relief column. Nothing now remains of these fortifications, but in the dry summer of 1964 an aerial photograph revealed the shape of the earthworks and of two of the star-shaped forts.

of Carisbrooke on the Isle of Wight, rebuilt in the 1590s lest a Spanish Armada should ever reach England. There were also a host of defence-works built in England and Scotland during the great Civil War of the 1640s: many of them are still there. However, even where a fortress has almost disappeared, there may be mounds and humps, or perhaps just marks in the crops, which reveal where the structures used to be. The pictures of Amiens show the extensive siege-works which were thrown up around the town in 1597; today, nothing can be seen on the ground itself, and yet from an aeroplane the pattern of the defences may still be partially revealed because crops tend to grow differently in soil which has been disturbed.

After learning what we can from nearby museums, castles, town ramparts and 'humps and bumps', we can look in books for further information about the soldiers of Renaissance Europe. A very large number of books were written about war

The title page from John Cruso, Militarie Instructions for the Cavall'rie, *printed at Cambridge in 1632. Cruso complained that previous writers on cavalry tactics 'had so written, as if none should read them but such as were alreadie skilfull in the art militarie'. He therefore set out to write a manual for beginners, lavishly illustrated (see the picture on page 21). It proved very popular.*

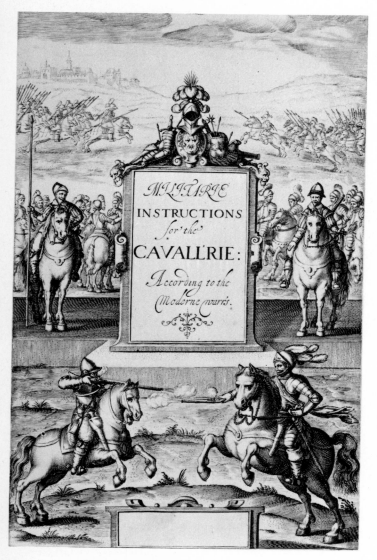

and warfare in the sixteenth and seventeenth centuries, and the best of them were illustrated. Since they were meant to explain to people who wanted to become army officers what sort of things soldiers did and how they did them, books like these are extremely useful and tell us a great deal about how soldiers were drilled, how they made camp, and how they used their weapons – although, as we shall see, many books were not always *quite* as clear as they might have been! A number of the illustrations in this book are taken from military writings of the time.

Another valuable type of contemporary evidence is provided by artists. War was a favourite subject of many painters and engravers, and many pictures managed to convey very effectively the hardship and brutality of the soldier's life. Look at the picture at the front of this book. It shows the troops of one army cutting the throats of their enemies in cold blood. Look also at the picture on page 22 by another artist, Pieter Snaeyers of Antwerp, which shows how ragged and dispirited soldiers could become in winter. However, neither pictures, nor books, nor museums can tell us what it *felt* like to be a soldier in those hundred years. For that we must turn to other sources.

We have famous authors like Cervantes from Spain and Von Grimmelshausen from Germany, both of whom served in the wars and both of whom wrote vivid books about the life of the ordinary soldier based on their own personal experience. Shorter, more numerous, and perhaps more reliable, there are the letters and other documents written by individual soldiers while they were on active service, recording events and situations as they actually occurred. Many of these eye-witness accounts of suffering and dissatisfaction are very moving documents, like the ones on page 10. You may find that your local Record Office has some letters like these. If so, they may be fairly easy to read (if the person who wrote the document was well-educated), or they may be difficult, if not impossible, to read (if written by an ordinary private who had perhaps

A collection of cannon balls and bullets of different sizes found on one of the ships of the Spanish Armada which sank off the Irish coast in 1588. It was excavated by divers in 1970. In the foreground are pistol, arquebus and musket balls (in ascending size); to the right are metal cannon balls; to the left stone cannon balls. All the balls are solid. The idea of filling them with gunpowder so that they would explode only came in after 1590.

Two examples of the documents produced by the misfortunes of war. Below is the petition (from Cheshire in England) of two local farm workers who had been hired to fight in Sir George Booth's Royalist rebellion in Cheshire in 1659. They were captured at the battle of Winnington Bridge on 23 August by the forces of the Protectorate. After the Restoration of the king in 1660 the unlucky soldiers tried to get some compensation for their suffering from those who had hired them.

In the transcription opposite, line endings are shown by diagonal strokes.

The second example is in Spanish and comes from the Netherlands in 1594. Again the soldiers are demanding money, this time from the government which employed them. They claim to be owed one hundred months' wages (an exaggeration), and they leave the government in no doubt about the consequences of abandoning them without pay any longer. The child-like writing makes the letter seem even more threatening. The sheet of paper was sent on to the central government in Spain to illustrate the low morale of the troops.

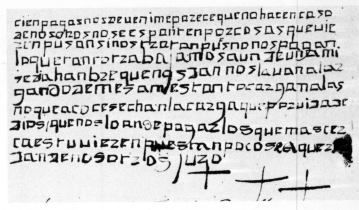

Transcription

They owe us a hundred pays and it seems to me that they don't care about us. Let them not be shocked at what they may see [if we revolt] since they treat us this way and don't pay us who work so hard. They even drag out from one month to the next the miserable hunger they impose upon us. They load up the donkey so much that they have to do it with kicks. By God's life I swear that those who are nearest must pay for it, since they take so little thought for us.

Transcription

To the Honourable his Majesties Justices
of Peace for Northwich Hundred The humble
Peticion of Edward Morton and William Gwenn most humbly
Sheweth. / .

That whereas your poore Peticioners beeing labouring men / were hyred by the inhabitants of Sandbach to serve for y^t [=that] place / in the last Engagement of the truly honourable S^r [=Sir] George / Booth ; and did therein with faith, and deligence, discharge their dutie / under the comand of the Worshipfull Collonel Manwaring untill / that upon the scattering of theire forces, they were taken at Winington / Bridg, and not receiveing any releife from them for whom they ser- / ved, did suffer extreame imprisonment, in greate miserie, which their / narrow fortunes were not sufficient to releeve ; but that through, and / by reason of soe chargeable an imprisonment ; & the losse of their time, they / were reduced to a woefull necessitie, & expectation of a certaine ruen [=ruin].

The premisses considered, your poore peticioners crave your Honours / gracious Order to the Constables of Sandbach aforesaid, that the / Inhabitants thereof may yeeld them, your poore peticioners such pay as / by other Townes hath bin allowed, to theire hyred soldiers, in the like Case, / that theire extreame want may bee remoued, their miserable life comforted ; / and your poore Peticioners (who now throw themselves at your Honours + / feete, as Objects of pittie) will euer pray as bounden for your / Honours health and happinesse. /

Three helmets from the 1570s in the Wallace Collection in London, one of the richest collections of arms and armour in Europe. They are real works of art, with beautiful decoration, and two have a special place for a plume. However, like the arms and armour of most other museums, they do not represent the poorly made, mass-produced articles worn by the rank-and-file in every army.

left school when he was only nine – or even earlier: many never went at all). Either way, if you take the trouble to study them carefully, old letters will almost certainly tell you something new.

Finally, there are the official records kept by each government concerning its armed forces. These include letters, accounts of money spent, muster-rolls, order-books, pay-sheets and other lists. All sorts of things connected with armies were written down: how much bread was supplied to the troops, how tall the soldiers were, how many of them died in service . . . These official papers have also provided a lot of the material included in this book.

1 The men and their weapons

What they looked like

The first thing that we need to know about the soldiers of the sixteenth and seventeenth centuries is what they looked like. From all the pictures of soldiers here you can see at once that they look different from the soldiers of today in almost every way. Probably the most striking thing about them is that they all have a moustache and a beard and many of them have long hair. This is no accident: it is the same in most of the other opposite and below left: *These three prints are taken from one of the most popular military drill-books of the seventeenth century, Jacob de Gheyn's* The Use of Weapons: Arquebus, Musket and Pike, *1607. Each picture was meant to show correct position and stance for soldiers doing drill with one of these three weapons. Each was also numbered, so the officer in charge of the drill could simply* call out the number and check in his book that everyone was doing the right thing.

below right: *A much later work, Jan Boxel,* A Picture of Arms Drill, *1673, shows that little had changed since de Gheyn's book. The method of teaching by numbered pictures was the same and only the dress of the soldier (and his hairstyle) is different.*

pictures in this book. It was believed in the early modern period that men looked fiercer with a lot of hair on their face. And perhaps they do.

The next striking thing – to our eyes at least – is that the troops were not dressed in any particular way, apart perhaps from body-guards on show at court. This too is no accident. It was argued that soldiers should be left free to choose their own clothes with plumes, doublets and breeches of whatever cut

These two roughly contemporary prints show the limits of drill during our period. On the left is a magnificently confident sergeant-major, carrying his halberd, the symbol of his authority. Behind him, his company is executing a complicated manoeuvre . . . but they are not marching in step ! On the right, the Dutch army is shown closing in on the castle of Wedde in Friesland in 1593. Again the Dutch are not shown marching in step, whether as a narrow column or as a square formation. The men at the bottom left of this picture are not soldiers at all but pioneers, labourers specially recruited to build fortifications and dig trenches. Here they are shown in action.

and colour they liked. They were thought more likely to fight cheerfully and bravely that way. Only in the 1630s did some armies begin to dress whole regiments alike in *uniforms*: the famous 'Blue Guards' of Gustavus Adolphus of Sweden, for example, or the even more famous red-coats of the New Model Army. In other armies the only way to distinguish the men of one side from their enemies was by the mark which everyone had to wear over their clothes. A scarf or a sash of a certain colour was the normal thing: red for Spain, blue for France and so on. These colours had been in use since at least the fourteenth century so every soldier (unless he was colour-blind!) would know what they meant.

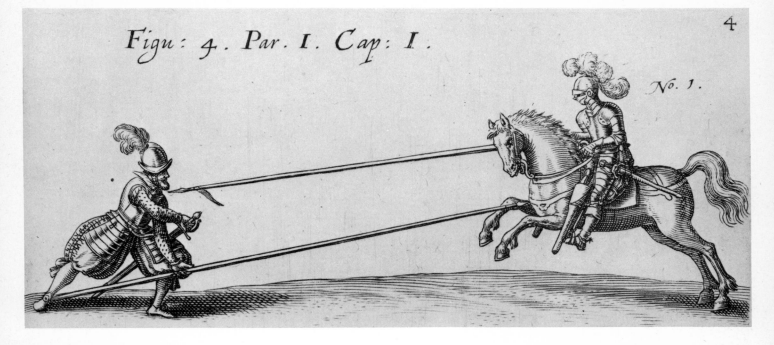

Figu: 4. Par. I. Cap: I.

Weapons

Everyone was expected to carry a sword and dagger at this time, but the pictures in this section show the two other main weapons carried by infantry soldiers: the pike and musket. They also show how they were used. The pike was the commonest weapon, even though its great length, anything between 15 and 20 feet (4.5–6 m), made it very difficult to manage. The diagrams here suggest some of the problems. The men in picture 10 overleaf are certainly having trouble! The pictures show the correct position for the pike when other foot-soldiers had to be attacked: the men advanced with their pikes pointed straight ahead, ready to jab them into the faces of their opponents. The position of the pike when used against cavalry was somewhat different. Then the pike was placed against its owner's heel and pointed at the chest of the advancing horse (whose rider is trying to give as good as he gets: not for nothing do both combatants wear armour). Normally, the pikemen fought in close formation, most often drawn up into a square with their weapons pointed outwards in every direction, forming something like a hedgehog or a porcupine. Few horsemen dared to attack a square of pikemen.

Although not nearly as unwieldy as the pike, the musket was by no means easy to use. It was slow. There were twenty-eight actions and several minutes were required to load and fire it.

15

*Parts of two sequences of illustrations from Wallhausen's
Military Prowess on Foot. As on page 12 each movement
is numbered, but this time there is a description in the text
of what the soldier should do. The most obvious features of
the pikeman's equipment are the large amount of armour he
had to wear, and the extremely clumsy length of his
weapon. In the sketches of the musketeer, note the slow-
match which must be kept alight all the time, and the
pouches of ammunition slung around the soldier's shoulder-
strap. It was not unknown for a man to blow himself up by
carelessly allowing his slow-match to go too near his
powder.*

A display of the arms and armour used by the Swiss infantry during the sixteenth century. Some wear armour that is burnished bright, others have it painted black; some point pikes at their opponents' faces, others wield halberds. The Swiss soldiers were famous for their courage and firmness in action. On the wall behind the soldiers is a picture of Swiss troops fighting, drawn by Hans Holbein (see also page 51 below).

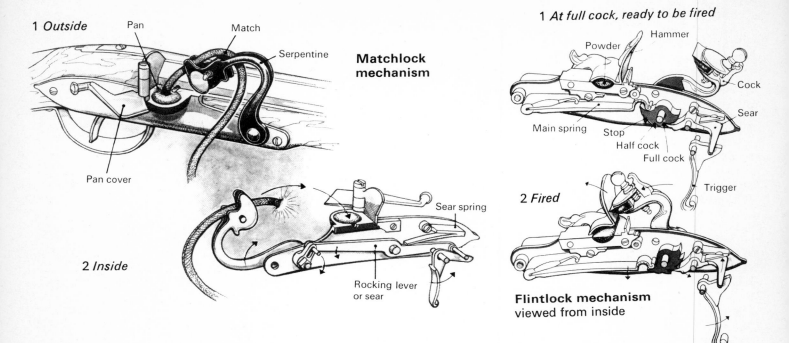

1 Outside

Pan — Match — Serpentine

Pan cover

Matchlock mechanism

2 Inside

Sear spring

Rocking lever or sear

1 At full cock, ready to be fired

Powder — Hammer — Cock — Sear

Main spring — Stop — Half cock — Full cock — Trigger

2 Fired

Flintlock mechanism viewed from inside

The firing sequence for the matchlock and flintlock muskets.

In the matchlock diagrams, (1) the serpentine is shown pressing the glowing slow-match onto the priming powder in the pan. In (2) the arrows indicate the lock motion in action.

The flintlock mechanism, which replaced the matchlock during the seventeenth century, is less risky; when the trigger is squeezed, the sear releases the stop so that the cock springs forward and the flint strikes the hammer. Only at this moment, as the hammer is knocked up, is the powder in the pan exposed to firing sparks.

right: An original musket being fired from its forked rest. The trigger has been pulled; the powder ignited. The exploding powder can be seen clearly as it leaves the barrel.

Musketeer meets horseman. Although the musket had a longer range than this, it took so long to reload that the musketeer only had time to fire once or twice before the cavalry was upon him. It was therefore prudent to wait until the last minute before firing; if he missed his mark, he was lost.

The musket was heavy, almost 20 pounds (9 kg) in weight, or about three times the weight of a modern rifle. It could only be fired from a forked rest. Besides his musket and its rest, each soldier had to carry

  his own powder-charges (in small pouches hanging from his shoulder-strap)
  a priming flask to hold the specially fine powder that was needed in the pan
  a length of slow-burning cord to fire the priming powder (and something to light the cord with)
  a piece of lead and a small mould with which to make bullets (every soldier had to make his own!)
  and so on.

The gun was fired by applying the 'match' to a small charge of powder in the firing pan, which in turn ignited the main charge in the barrel. If aimed accurately, the musket ball, often an inch or more (3 cm) in diameter, could kill a man up to a quarter of a mile (or 400 m) away. But, of course, with a weapon that was so complicated to handle, things were always going wrong. With too little powder the bullet would fall short; with too much the barrel would blow up in the musketeer's face. Even if the main charge was absolutely right, the powder in the firing pan might explode without setting off the powder in the barrel. (Hence the expression 'a flash in the pan'.) Also, a careless musketeer might let the bullet roll out of the barrel before he fired! Most common of all, however, the match went out at the critical moment, especially in rain, and the musketeer was left defenceless. This is no doubt why we see that in the picture on pages 52–3, the battle of Nördlingen, the musketeers kept very close to their pikemen, so that they could run behind them for protection.

The musket was therefore treated as something of a joke among some old soldiers, who said its only value was to scare inexperienced enemies with the noise of the powder exploding! But they were wrong. Military experts were always trying to find ways of making it more manageable, more reliable, and more accurate. In the early seventeenth century it was discovered that the 'match' could be replaced by a flint which made a spark when it struck the steel hammer on the firing pan, set fire to the powder there, and thus exploded the whole charge. The 'matchlock' was gradually replaced by the 'flintlock' and the musket began to play a decisive role in European warfare.

All firearms, however, were taken seriously by the cavalry troopers. In the sixteenth century, as in the Middle Ages, the horsemen relied on heavy armour to protect them against stray shots and pike thrusts. As the accuracy and fire-power of the musket increased, it became clear that this was no longer enough. Against pikemen, the cavalry could use horse carbines, or long pistols, kept in special holsters at the saddle (they are clearly shown in the illustration on page 21). But there was no defence against artillery and musketry: a body of horsemen moving slowly in full armour made an easy target.

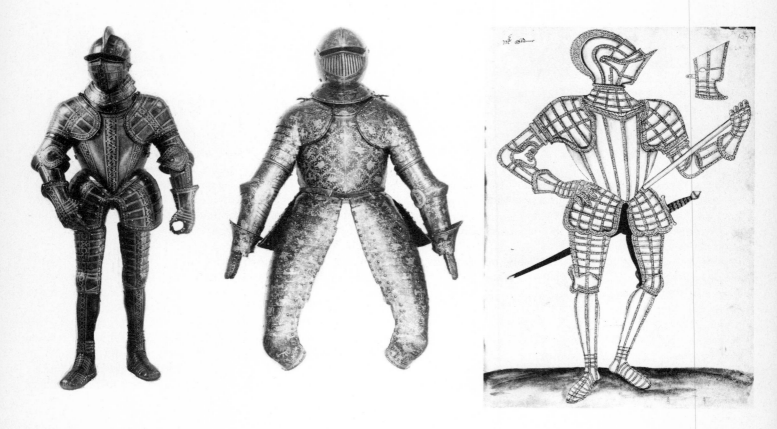

The complete suit of armour on the left was for ceremonial occasions, and was made c. 1600 for Lord Buckhurst in the Royal Armoury at Greenwich; it weighs just over 70 pounds (32 kg). The second suit of armour was only for use on horseback; it was made in Italy in the 1620s for the Duke of Savoy, and it weighs around 60 pounds (27 kg). The drawing on the right is a complete suit very similar to the first photo, and was designed by an English Court artist in the 1600s.

Armour

Although a number of magnificent suits of armour have survived from the sixteenth century, most of the specimens were meant only for show, not for action, like the superb suits shown in this selection, engraved in gold with swirling patterns from head to toe. One of the very finest and most complete examples of sixteenth-century armour to have survived, ironically, was made for the Master of the Artillery of France, the man in charge of the great guns which made armour largely useless. He would never have dreamed of going into battle with it on!

One answer to the invention of bigger guns was for the cavalry to move faster and thus provide a more difficult target for the gunners. With a really fast charge, it was found that only two rounds could be fired before the cavalry closed home. The horsemen therefore left their heavy armour behind,

left: *The cavalry did not always use lances. Sometimes they used either carbines or large pistols especially made for use on horseback. This picture from Cruso's manual of 1632 (see page 8) shows cavalry fighting cavalry.*

below: *A sturdy 'lobster pot', made in England during the mid-seventeenth century. Mass-produced and made for use not decoration, it protected the head, nose, ears and neck of the cavalry trooper from sword blows. The screw on the nose guard allowed it to be raised and lowered.*

keeping just a breast- and back-plate, and sometimes also armour to protect the upper legs, known as 'tassets'. You can see these tassets in the second suit of armour on the opposite page and also in the picture above of a cavalry charge.

Everyone also wore a helmet in action. The most famous helmet of the later sixteenth century was the 'morion', three of which are shown on page 11; in the seventeenth century it was replaced for cavalry by the 'lobster pot' which was worn by horsemen on both sides during the English Civil War. For weapons, the new-style cavalry relied on swords rather than lances or pistols, and they aimed to make the maximum impact on their foes. The tactics shown in the print of cavalry using large pistols were fast becoming out of date.

Whether they are wearing armour, riding a horse, or carrying a pike, you may have noticed that all the soldiers in the pictures so far look neat, healthy and alert. In real life, however, they were not always like that. On some occasions, it is true, soldiers looked like princes. In 1567 a Frenchman observed a Spanish army on the move and wrote: 'There were 10,000 foot soldiers, all hardened veterans, so well-equipped with both clothes and weapons (many of them inlaid with gold) that one would have supposed that they were captains rather than ordinary soldiers. One would have said that they were princes, such was the pride, dignity and arrogance with which they marched.'

No army remained like that for long. Sometimes the soldiers were forced to serve barefoot, scarcely clothed. It is true that most men received a free set of garments when they joined the army, but these soon wore out on active service and it might be months and even years before a new set was provided. In 1646 an officer of the English Parliamentary army in Cheshire

Pieter Snaeyers was a military artist who lived in Antwerp. This picture shows the Spanish army's encampments around Aire-sur-le-Lys in 1641. The fortifications of the besiegers are very like Henry IV's earthworks around Amiens, shown on page 6.

complained that his men had 'not wherewithall to cover their nakedness nor a penny mony in their pockets; truely I confesse, if I had not bin an eye witness I should hardly have believed it'. At about the same time, in 1641, a similarly grim account was given of some soldiers in the Spanish army on active service in the Netherlands. This time the hardships were described in a picture, shown here. We see them with their feet bare, scarcely covered as they march through the snow. Small wonder that one of the soldiers (under the tree, in the centre) is dying: the chaplain is hearing his last confession.

Even a 'realistic' picture like this fails to tell us the whole truth about the soldiers of the sixteenth and seventeenth centuries. For one thing, the picture does not tell us how short most soldiers would have seemed to present-day eyes. Even a crack regiment like the Royal Guards of Louis XIV, troops chosen especially for their height, did not have one soldier who was taller than 5 feet 9 inches (1.75 m). Indeed there were only ten men, out of 3,500, who were more than 5 feet 8 inches (1.73 m). The explanation is that people in Europe then were on average much smaller in size than we are today, perhaps as much as 1 foot shorter. Not one person in thirty, in the population as a whole, was over 5 feet tall.

The soldiers, and civilians too, would also seem 'ugly' to us. They were often heavily disfigured both by fighting and by disease. Whenever the records of an army note the appearance of its soldiers we find that a very large number of men bore the marks of smallpox, had no teeth, or had a growth of some sort on their face. With little medical care available, this is not surprising. Most soldiers also bore the traces of wounds suffered in action: eyes torn out, pike or sword scars, missing arms and legs. Others were so badly injured that they were unable to continue in service. Sadly, some were unable to earn a living at all and were reduced to begging in order to survive. We have to remember that although some soldiers and their officers passed through every campaign unscathed and looked neat and alert like the men shown in the pictures at the beginning of this chapter, many other soldiers did not. Every army left behind it a trail of human lives wrecked or wasted in battle.

Where the soldiers came from

Armies nowadays are almost always raised in the same country for which they are fighting. During the wars of this century the German army was composed overwhelmingly of Germans, the French army of Frenchmen and so on. It is considered safer that way: people who are fighting for the defence of their own countries, their families and possessions, are more likely to fight well. But in earlier times, things were different.

The problem was that no European government could afford to pay for a large, professional army all the time. In peacetime, almost all soldiers were demobilized in order to save money.

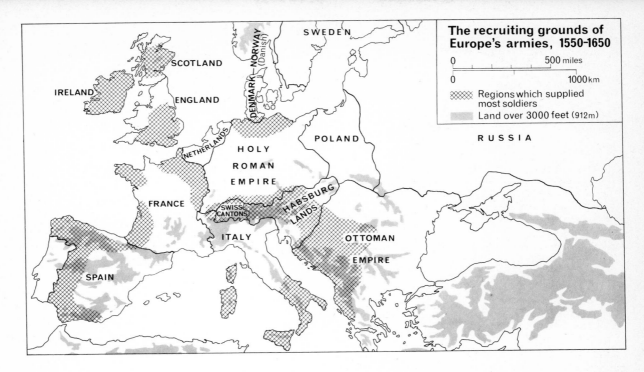

The recruiting grounds of
Europe's armies, 1550-1650

Regions which supplied
most soldiers

Land over 3000 feet (912m)

Therefore, when war broke out, each government had to recruit its forces from scratch and it had to do so quickly. The best thing was to find men who had fought before in some earlier war and who therefore had some idea of how to use a pike or musket. Some of these veterans would doubtless be found locally (unless there had been a very long period of peace) but almost certainly there would not be enough. The rest of the experienced troops would have to be found abroad. The regions which supplied most of the soldiers for Europe's armies were the mountainous areas, and the regions near to political frontiers which had frequently been battle grounds.

There were a number of areas of Europe which, in effect, 'exported' trained soldiers: the southern states of Germany, the Swiss cantons, and the Balkans. These mountainous lands with poor soil always had more people than they could feed, and a tradition grew up that active young men unable to find anything to do at home went off to join an army, any army, in order to earn some money. Sometimes men were recruited by a local nobleman who would build up a whole company, even a regiment, and then hire it out to any government which

was prepared to pay for it; sometimes the men went off individually to search for an army which required their services. Before long German, Swiss and 'Albanian' troops (from the Balkans) were to be found in almost every army in Europe, fighting alongside the men raised locally.

However, these professional soldiers who would fight for any master who would pay them, 'mercenaries' as they were known, were seldom totally trusted. On a number of occasions a battle was lost because the mercenaries refused to fight until they were paid; at other times mercenaries changed sides because they were offered more money. It was therefore rare to find more than a third, or at most a half, of an army made up of mercenaries. The rest were new recruits raised in the lands of the government fighting the war. Although there was sometimes conscription in those days, and also 'pressing of men' (that is kidnapping them and taking them away to the wars against their will), normally it was enough to call for volunteers. An officer and a couple of veterans toured a town or a group of villages beating a drum. They offered a cash reward, food, and the promise of future wages to all who would join the army

Enlistment: A soldier joins up in Germany in the 1570s. The captain pays the man his first month's wages; the company clerk enters his name on the list. Below, soldiers join up in Germany in the 1630s. Only the style of the soldiers' dress has changed.

for the duration of the present war. The names of those who accepted this offer were written down on a list (they 'enlisted') and they received their reward in public. The two pictures on this page, one from the 1570s and one from the 1630s, show just such a moment: the recruiting captain is paying a new recruit his enlistment money.

It was recognized that the number of volunteers varied according to the time of year. At times when there was little work (and therefore little money to be earned) the offer of cash now and wages to follow could seem very tempting. On the other hand in summer, when everyone was busy harvesting the corn, hardly any soldiers could be found. It was therefore necessary for the recruiting officers to adopt other methods. Men who were in gaol for their misbehaviour might be offered a pardon if they agreed to serve in the army for a fixed period.

Men who were too idle or too feeble or too drunk to gain their living in any other way would be accepted. Finally, a sort of conscription was introduced, forcing civilians to join up whether they wanted to or not. William Shakespeare has left us a vivid description of this system in operation during the reign of Queen Elizabeth I, in *King Henry IV*, Part II.

A recruiting captain, Sir John Falstaff, and his assistant, Corporal Bardolph, arrive in a Gloucestershire village which has been told to provide four men for the wars. The local magistrates, Shallow and Silence by name, have collected five potential recruits for Falstaff to choose from: Bullcalf, a bell-ringer, Feeble, a tailor, and three of the local unemployed, Mouldy, Shadow and Wart. A fine crowd they were! Feeble was trembling with fear, Wart had legs like pins and was clearly too weak to carry a musket (let alone fire it), and Shadow was so thin that, said Falstaff, the enemy might as well shoot at the edge of a penknife. The other two men soon realize what is about to happen and they take Corporal Bardolph aside:

'Be my friend', says Bullcalf the bellringer. 'I'd rather be hanged than be a soldier. Here's two pounds to let me off.'

'It's a deal', says Bardolph.

Now Mouldy tries the same trick:

'Be my friend', he says. 'For my wife's sake let me off too. Here's another two pounds.'

'It's a deal', says Bardolph.

Feeble the tailor will have none of this, however. He may be frightened but he knows his duty:

'I care not', he says. 'A man can die but once and no man is too good to serve his prince.'

So Feeble, Shadow and Wart, the unfit men, are conscripted, and the able-bodied men are left behind.

By such methods, very large armies could be collected. Philip IV of Spain had 300,000 men under arms in 1625 (although they were not all in the same place). Gustavus

> *Bul.* Good Master Corporate *Bardolph*, stand my friend, and heere is foure *Harry* tenne shillings in French Crownes for you : in very truth, sir, I had as lief be hang'd sir, as goe : and yet, for mine owne part, sir, I do not care ; but rather, becaufe I am vnwilling, and for mine owne part, haue a desire to stay with my friends : else, sir, I did not care, for thine owne part, so much.
>
> *Bard.* Go-too: stand aside.
>
> *Mould.* And good Master Corporall Captaine, for my old Dames sake, stand my friend : shee hath no body to doe any thing about her, when I am gone : and she is old, and cannot helpe her selfe : you shall haue fortie, sir.
>
> *Bard.* Go-too: stand aside.
>
> *Feeble.* I care not, a man can die but once : wee owe a death. I will neuer beare a base minde : if it be my destinie, so : if it be not, so : no man is too good to serue his Prince : and let it goe which way it will, he that dies this yeere, is quit for the next.
>
> *Bard.* Well said, thou art a good fellow.
>
> *Feeble.* Nay, I will beare no base minde.
>
> *Falst.* Come sir, which men shall I haue?
>
> *Shal.* Foure of which you please.
>
> *Bard.* Sir, a word with you : I haue three pound, to free *Mouldie* and *Bull-calfe*.
>
> *Falst.* Go-too: well.

Enlistment again: in England Sir John Falstaff conscripts four soldiers for the wars during the 1590s. Here the soldiers offer the captain money not *to be taken into the army!*

25

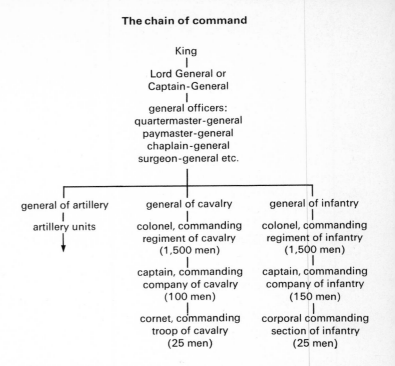

```
                           King
                            |
                   Lord General or
                   Captain-General
                            |
                   general officers:
                   quartermaster-general
                   paymaster-general
                   chaplain-general
                   surgeon-general etc.
                            |
     _____
    |                       |                                |
general of artillery   general of cavalry          general of infantry
    |                       |                                |
artillery units        colonel, commanding         colonel, commanding
    |                    regiment of cavalry          regiment of infantry
    ↓                      (1,500 men)                   (1,500 men)
                            |                                |
                       captain, commanding          captain, commanding
                        company of cavalry           company of infantry
                          (100 men)                     (150 men)
                            |                                |
                       cornet, commanding          corporal commanding
                        troop of cavalry              section of infantry
                          (25 men)                      (25 men)
```

Adolphus of Sweden had 120,000 soldiers in Germany in 1631, and his enemies probably had as many again. With such enormous concentrations of men, it was essential to organize them into smaller units and to establish a chain of command which linked the Lord General with the most insignificant private in the army. In the first place, every soldier belonged to a 'section' or 'squadron' of about twenty-five men under a corporal. He also belonged, with his section comrades, to a company of about 150 men under a captain, and to a regiment of about 1,500 men under a colonel. Sometimes the regiment was stationed in a garrison town as a more or less independent unit; sometimes several regiments were grouped together as a field army under a general. In both cases a number of administrative officers were added to the fighting troops to keep them fit and fed: doctors, surgeons and chaplains were provided to care for their physical and mental health; quartermasters, paymasters and supply officers looked after their bodily needs.

On the whole the officers were gentlemen, and they normally came from the same region as their men (indeed, as we have seen, they often did their own recruiting). Usually they served in the ranks for a brief period to gain first-hand experience of the problems and conditions of military life, but the 'gentlemen-rankers' were always treated as a class apart. They were given special privileges like extra pay and extra rations, and exempted from the more menial chores of camp existence. It was, as a rule, impossible for ordinary soldiers of humble birth to rise above the rank of corporal or sergeant (the 'non-commissioned' officers). The army was always socially divided. And yet all the soldiers—officers, gentleman-rankers and men—were in a sense members of the same family. When there was a shortage of food they all went hungry; when there was fighting they all risked death or disablement; when there was victory they all shared the triumph and the spoils. As we shall see, army life, though unequal in some ways, was equal in others.

2 Life in the ranks

Thanks to our different sources of information, we have a fair idea of the feel and sight and sound and smell of military life in the sixteenth and seventeenth centuries. We know a lot about the hardships and the sorrows, the consolations and the achievements of many soldiers of different nations. At most times, for almost everyone, life was hard. And, as you might expect, it got harder the further you were down the ladder of promotion.

Lodgings, food and pay

When King Henry VIII of England invaded France in 1513, three large wagons were needed to carry just the tents he was to live in on campaign. When erected, the royal tents covered 4,000 square feet (372 square m) – equal in size to a football pitch. Another wagon carried the king's pride and joy: a 'house of wood' made of special sections which could be put together and taken down again at each stop on the march.

In fact, few armies in the sixteenth century were led on campaign by their king in person, and anyway the extravagant Henry VIII was by no means typical of European rulers, but the paraphernalia which accompanied him in 1513 does illustrate the point that the standard of comfort which senior officers enjoyed was very different from that of the common soldiers. The pictures overleaf reveal one principal difference: officers in most armies slept in bell-tents of double canvas

The English army prepares to repel a French invasion in 1544. Notice the old-style bowmen beside the cannon on the left and the latest type of fortification, the bastions of Portsmouth castle. Henry VIII, mounted on the right, looks on with confidence.

This engraved sketch of Henry VIII of England's encampment at Marquison, near Boulogne in France, in 1544, is a copy. It was made in 1788 from one of a set of original paintings which were then to be found at Lord Montague's country house at Cowdray in Sussex. Subsequently the house was burnt out, and all that remain of the pictures are these fine, detailed engravings.

28

(one 'skin' inside and one outside to keep out the cold better).

You can see the different types of tent in the drawing opposite. The soldiers are actually striking camp: pulling down their officers' tents, square or round, large or small, and folding them up. Some of them seem to be rather better at taking tents down than others! The ordinary soldiers did not have tents of their own to take down. It was said, by the officers of course, that if the soldiers were allowed to sleep in tents there would be too much baggage. The privates were therefore expected, in the official phrase, 'to find their own lodgings'.

Often this meant that men had to sleep in the open under a

How to erect a camp: tents for the officers, makeshift huts for the men; guns and weapons around the outside of the camp, firebrakes between the rows of tents. Look at the incidental details: soldiers playing cards on the right; the women cooking, children playing, the man on a stretcher in the centre; the bullock about to be slaughtered at top left and the man drinking out of an enormous beer-mug at bottom left.

hedgerow, and we know that during a winter campaign many soldiers actually froze to death as they slept. The veterans, however, knew how to look after themselves and generally avoided this fate. If they were near trees they cut down branches to make a rough frame, then they covered the frame with straw, clods of earth, or a canvas sheet. If there were any empty houses about, they tore down the doors and shutters and anything else made of wood which might be used as a part of their hut. The second picture, first published in 1573, shows a number of soldiers in the act of erecting their shelters from these materials.

Actually a soldier could be warmer in a small home-made shelter like this than in a large tent or a deserted house. A hardy and enterprising Welsh soldier of Henry VIII, Elis Gruffudd, wrote in his campaign diary that he awoke one winter morning, having slept 'as snug as a small pig' in the hut he had made, to hear a man in the next tent exclaim: 'Ah, sirs, if I had known at the beginning of the night that there would be as much frost and snow as this I would not have taken so much trouble to search my shirt for lice, but I should have hung it out in the wind and let them die of cold as we shall do if we stay here any longer!' Nevertheless, many a frozen soldier, as he lay on the ground in his humble hut, must have cast an envious glance at the vast marquees which housed the commander-in-chief and his senior officers.

Life was a little more comfortable for the rank and file when the campaign ended and they moved into winter-quarters or garrison duty. Big barracks, where soldiers normally live today, were not built in Europe until the early eighteenth century. Before that time, each soldier was assigned a 'billet', that is a household in the village or town where he was stationed. There he, and the other soldiers allotted to the same house, had the right to free food and a free bed (or part of a bed; normally two or three soldiers were expected to share the same bed). This was fine for the soldiers: they were able to live for nothing. But it could mean starvation for the civilians on whom they were billeted. Poor workmen or peasants did not have enough extra food to satisfy two or three hungry soldiers as well as

their own family. Disagreements soon arose between the householders and the soldiers.

Sometimes the brutality of the soldiers was encouraged by their officers. Thus in 1579, during Queen Elizabeth's Irish wars, the commander of her forces in Ulster, Sir Humphrey Gilbert, made it a habit that whenever he made a raid 'into the enemy's country, he killed man, woman and child, and spoiled, wasted and burned . . . all that he might, leaving nothing of the enemy's in safety which he could possibly waste or consume . . . The killing of them by the sworde was the way to kill the men of war by famine, who in flight would often save themselves', by taking refuge with the local population. This ruthless policy was usually only employed in a situation where, as in Ireland, an alien government was trying to impose its authority on a largely hostile population which normally tended to shelter any rebels. It was felt that if rebels were able to live among the local inhabitants like fish in water, the way to kill the fish was to dry up the water.

Not surprisingly, with behaviour like this, popular feeling against soldiers often ran high. The comments of two writers are fairly typical: Barnaby Rich wrote in 1578, 'If you would call a tyrant, a blasphemer, a murderer, a robber, a spoiler, a deflowerer, an oppressor in one short name, you may call him by the name of *soldier*'. In 1579 Geoffrey Gates wrote, 'Soldiers are so venemous a brood to their native country that they are rather to be vomited out of the bulk of the commonwealth than to be nourished by the same'.

Nor did civilians always stop at words to express their hatred of the soldiers. Sometimes the soldiers billeted on a village behaved so outrageously that the whole civilian population got together and made war on any troops in the neighbourhood. This may seem surprising. It could hardly happen today, but in those times most civilians were nearly as well armed as the soldiers. They had axes, daggers and often guns too. There were occasions on which a hundred soldiers at a time

Two soldiers with their mistresses (and children) have come, un-invited, to eat and drink at the home of a peasant along their way. The peasants look on, apparently helpless, as the soldiers demand more drink. Notice that the soldiers, and their families, are dressed in silks and lace.

They have, however, left their weapons behind and the out-raged peasants, plainly dressed but armed with wood-axes and pitch-forks, rush in and murder the unwanted guests. These two paintings by the Dutch artist, David Vinckeboons, were made in the 1620s.

were ambushed, or murdered as they slept, by the local people they had mistreated.

Things were not often as bad as this, though. At most times the soldiers were provided with a reasonable quantity of food and drink by their hosts, and the government reduced the amount of taxes to be paid by the host in compensation. At other times the government provided food to the troops directly. This was always necessary if the soldiers had to go to sea for any reason. Aboard the Swedish warship *Vasa*, which sank in 1628 just after it left Stockholm harbour, large quantities of bread and other rations were found, all ready to be issued day by day to the men on board. The soldiers and crew were divided into groups of about eight. Each group had its own small wooden casket, containing eight earthenware bowls, a larger wooden bowl, some spoons and a knife. The men ate together using these utensils, although no doubt fingers were even more important. They were also allowed to drink 6 pints of beer every day. This may seem rather a large quantity to us, but the men on board needed every drop because they ate so much heavily salted food and had little or no fresh water to quench their thirst.

We find much the same thing on the ships of the Spanish Armada, equipped at the opposite end of Europe and wrecked off the coast of Ireland in the autumn of 1588. Underwater archaeologists have rediscovered these wrecks and among the finds are communal bowls, spoons and forks and barrels for storing food and drink.

With their basic bodily needs of food, clothing and shelter taken care of, the soldiers not on active service could settle down to a fairly leisurely life. As we shall see later, there was not much arms-drill or 'square-bashing', because few thought it important to march in step; and even less target practice, because powder and shot were considered too expensive to be 'wasted' when there was no enemy to shoot at. Without uniforms there were no buttons to clean or boots to polish.

In the case of the wrecked ships of the Spanish Armada, the sea has pounded away most of the vessel itself. All that remains is, in most cases, the metal weapons (especially the bronze and iron guns) and again the everyday objects aboard. The picture below shows a large wooden bowl, measuring 18 inches (46 cm) across, used by the crew of the Trinidad Valencera *which went down off County Donegal in Ireland. The photograph appears a little blurred because it was taken in the sea while the bowl was still on the bottom, just as it had come to rest when the ship went down.*

Not needing to spend time in these unrewarding pursuits, which take up so much of the modern soldier's day in peace-time, most soldiers were left with a great deal of time on their hands. And of course this was the great attraction of military life. No one joined up simply to starve and get killed. The picture on page 29 shows soldiers engaged in drinking, playing cards, dice and other games, and courting local ladies. The same activities figure prominently in the picture above painted by the Netherlands artist Pieter Brueghel in 1562, only this time the ever present threat of sudden death in action is emphasized.

It was not only the enemy which interfered with the soldier's leisure; there was also the lack of money. Not that the soldier's wages were inadequate. On the contrary, they were considerably higher than those of a farm labourer or unskilled town worker. The problem was that they were never paid on time.

Most governments always delayed paying their troops for as long as possible. Whole months could go by without a soldier seeing a penny of his pay. The New Model Army in England was owed about four months' back-pay when the first civil war ended in 1647; the Spanish army in the Netherlands in 1576 was owed between three and six *years* of overdue wages! Not unnaturally, these troops mutinied in protest, refusing to fight until they were paid. Eventually such 'strike action' was successful, but only for those who mutinied: governments could never afford to pay all their troops all the time and so on the whole it was the units which made the most trouble which got the most pay!

Only gradually was it realized that (as Napoleon later put it) 'An army marches on its stomach'. Not until the mid-seventeenth century did governments concentrate on providing

A rough watercolour sketch from the mid-sixteenth century showing an army on the march: guns, baggage, livestock and camp-followers in the middle; infantry and cavalry on the outside. It was a good idea to take one's food along 'on the hoof' in case the enemy had devastated the countryside through which an army had to pass.

their soldiers with food rather than with pay. By 1650 men in most armies were getting at least their daily bread. One 3-pound loaf every two days, made from mixed rye and wheat flour, became the standard ration of troops all over Europe. Today it may not seem much; but in early modern times it was more than most civilians could expect regularly.

Camp-followers and family

The splendid picture here of an army on the march shows that the soldiers of early modern Europe never went very far by themselves. In the middle of the infantry, the cavalry and the siege-guns, march orderly columns of women. One has her belongings on her head, others carry a knapsack (or is it a baby?). All have walking sticks to help them over the rough ground. Alongside them are children, mules, cattle (to kill and eat as necessary) and baggage-carts piled high with possessions, tents and equipment.

The picture gives some idea of just how many carts and camp-followers there were in each army. Quite often only half an 'army' were genuine soldiers: the rest were women, children and servants, and sometimes the camp-followers outnumbered the fighting men. All of them had to be fed and most of them wanted transport of some sort. An army of 5,300 Spanish soldiers marching from the Netherlands to Italy in 1577 demanded rations for 20,000 persons, or three camp-followers to every soldier. The expedition's baggage weighed 2,600 tons and it took 15 asses, 118 small mules and 365 large mules to carry it all. Some fifty years later, little had changed. A Dutch parson who saw a Spanish column marching to war in 1622 threw up his hands in horror. 'Such a long tail on such a small body has never been seen', he wrote. 'Such a small army with so many carts, baggage horses, nags, sutlers, lackeys, women, children, and a rabble which numbered far more than the army itself.'

In armies which were mobilized for a long time, where soldiers were recruited young and grew old in the service, many of the troops got married and had a family. The army became the 'home' of large numbers of women and children. They had no other. During the great war which raged in central Europe between 1618 and 1648, the Thirty Years War, each of the main armies as it moved about from one battle or siege to the next became a vast moving city with its own community life. There were shops, services and families, all defended by walls of iron – the weapons of its soldiers. When the war ended, many of the inhabitants of these mobile cities suddenly became 'homeless' for the camp was the only life they knew. A famous story was written about one camp-wife who did not

know what to do when she tried to return to civilian life during the German wars. It was called 'Mother Courage'. Recently it was made into a play.

Life for the soldier's wife was just as hard as it was for the soldier. Apart from cooking and looking after her children, she usually had to wash and mend and sew and clean for others in order to raise a little extra money for her family. If her husband was killed in battle her only hope was to marry again. 'Mother Courage' married eight soldiers and all but one of them met their death in action. If the husband of a camp-wife was defeated in battle, her life too might be forfeit since often the camp of a vanquished army fell into the hands of the victors and it was not uncommon for all the people found there to have their throats cut. If she was spared, she would automatically become the wife or the servant of one of the conquerors.

Drill and discipline

When you try to imagine a regiment marching, you probably think of neat ranks of soldiers, arranged in long lines, all in step, all dressed alike. We have already seen that the soldiers of sixteenth-century Europe wore no standard uniform. In fact they knew little about drill either. Plenty of books were written about how it should be done, but few soldiers ever learned.

Most armies needed only a small number of essential commands. Most of them, like 'advance your pikes' or 'follow your leader', were given by word of mouth, but some others were given by drum beat. The trouble with orders given on the drum was that, although easier to hear, they could be misunderstood. The English army therefore had only five different orders of this kind: 'advance', 'retreat', 'march', 'to arms' and 'form up'. Drums, fifes or pipes were also used then, as today, to help the soldiers to march in time together – even if out of step, as in the engraving here. This was not thought to be important in the sixteenth century, and quite often the military

musicians became more adventurous and played lively tunes and jigs so that, according to one English writer, the men were 'dancing and leaping' along, not proceeding in orderly ranks!

Of course, the dancing and leaping had to stop when the army came within sight of the enemy. The general then had to decide how to draw up his men for battle. In the sixteenth century this was relatively simple: the troops were drawn up in depth on a narrow front, infantry in the middle, cavalry on the wings and the field artillery either in front or, more usually, at the sides. When the general had made all ready, a certain number of experienced men, mainly musketeers and known as 'the forlorn hope', were sent well forward to skirmish with the enemy and, it was hoped, provoke a general engagement.

A bird's eye view of the battle of Naseby, just before the fighting began on 14 June 1645. The New Model Army is drawn up in the foreground in straight lines; the royalists are facing them in equally good order. Prince Rupert's cavalry faces Ireton's horse on the left; Cromwell's Ironsides are on the right. The 'forlorn hope' of the Parliamentarians is clearly shown in front of the main ranks, while King Charles himself rides before his army. The battle lasted several hours. Prince Rupert's cavalry began by driving off Ireton's horse in confusion, while Cromwell's men on the other flank eventually defeated their opponents. In the centre, the royalists steadily gained ground. The issue was decided, however, by the return of Cromwell's victorious horsemen, who rode down King Charles's infantry. By the time Prince Rupert's men returned, the battle was over; the king's forces were defeated and, as it turned out, the war was decided. Charles I surrendered less than a year later, having failed to assemble another army.

You can still visit the battlefield of Naseby in Northamptonshire just south of Market Harborough.

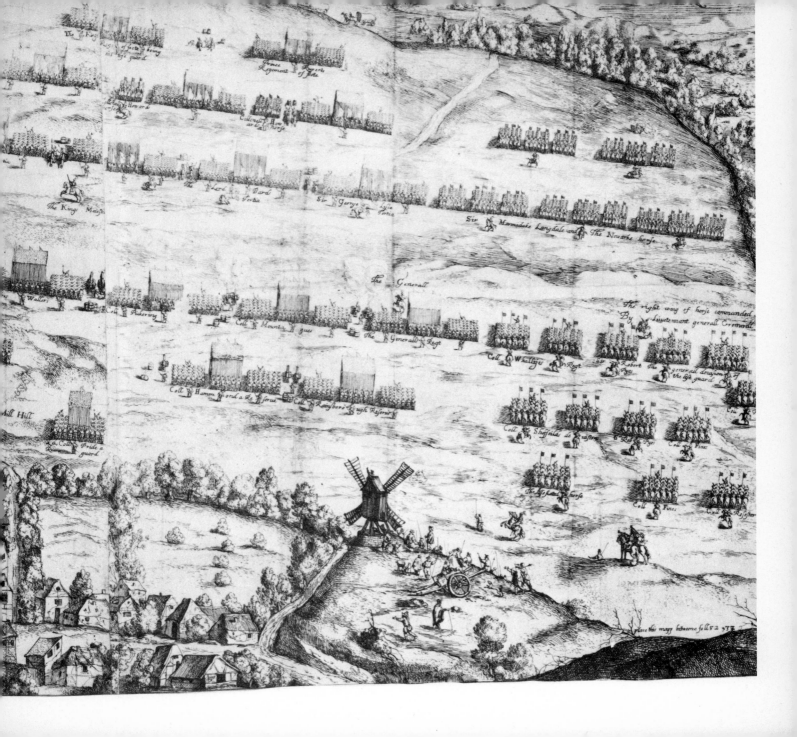

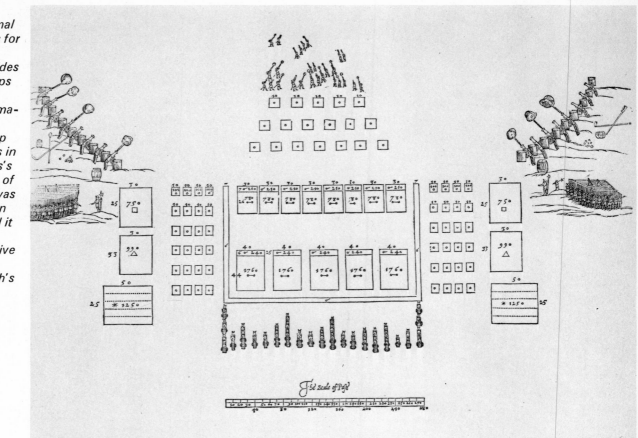

This diagram shows the normal layout of forces for battle: artillery placed to the sides and all the troops grouped into rectangular formations to form a narrow but deep front. It appears in Leonard Digges's military treatise of 1579. Digges was a mathematician by training, and it was only later that he saw active service (with Queen Elizabeth's army in the Netherlands).

In the sixteenth century the course of a battle from positions like those above was fairly predictable. The musketeers, standing in semi-circles or in two ranks (one kneeling and the other firing over their heads), poured fire into their opponents until the whole line advanced and the 'push of pike' began. According to one military writer, the men went forward 'carrying their pikes firmly with the points full in their enemy's faces', making 'rumours and shoutings, sometimes running with violence', blowing pipes and trumpets, beating drums and firing cannon. The more noise the better, according to this writer, since it 'wonderfully troubles and fears the hearts of the adversaries'. The small cavalry units had no part in all this. They were used only to attack the musketeers of the 'forlorn

hope' or to ride down the enemy after they had been defeated. If there was a head-on confrontation between the horsemen on one side and the horsemen on the other, it was normally a matter of firing pistols at each other (as in the picture on page 21) and riding away again to fight another day. The decisive weapon in most battles of the later sixteenth century was the pike.

This battle-pattern began to change in the seventeenth century. The number of musketeers increased, and the number of pikemen began to decline. Since horsemen were more effective against the slow-firing musketeers, the size of the cavalry contingent also grew. Many of the great battles of the English Civil War or of the German Thirty Years War therefore

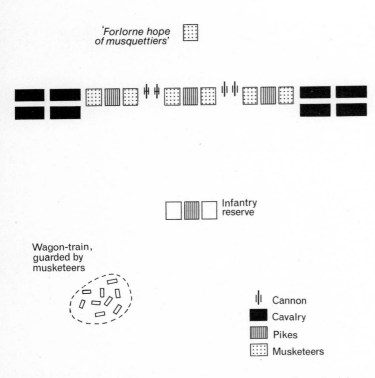

A schematic representation of the Parliamentary army at the battle of Naseby (1645) showing an entirely different concept from that shown on page 38. Here the front is wide and shallow, the artillery is in among the infantry and the cavalry is on the wings. The diagram is based on the engraving of the battle of Naseby on pages 36-7.

'Forlorne hope of musquettiers'

Infantry reserve

Wagon-train, guarded by musketeers

| | Cannon
Cavalry
Pikes
Musketeers

opened with a massed cavalry charge. It was often decisive. The cavalry went into battle on the wings, drawn up in three lines; the infantry too was drawn up in three lines with the musketeers in front. The second battle diagram, based on a book published in 1647, shows that the musketeers clearly outnumber the pikemen. In close combat they used their guns like clubs against the skulls of their enemies. The bayonet was not invented until the end of the seventeenth century.

However, these new fashions in fighting were not adopted by European soldiers everywhere. Spanish, Portuguese, English, French and Dutch soldiers were engaged in wars all over the world: in Asia, India, Africa and America. In all these areas

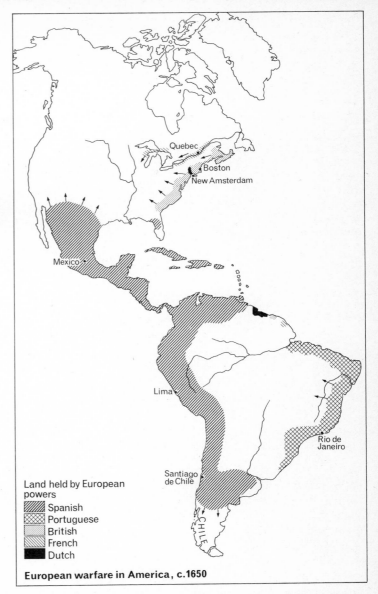

Land held by European powers
Spanish
Portuguese
British
French
Dutch

European warfare in America, c.1650

Except in Mexico, European settlements at the time shown on this map were confined to the coastal plains and the river valleys of the continent. European influence beyond this was represented by raids and punitive expeditions undertaken at measured intervals.

This sketch of 1613 shows a seventeenth-century battle, American style. The French explorer Champlain, with two European assistants, leads his Indian allies against the Iroquois.

they were heavily outnumbered by the native enemy. The illustration here shows Samuel de Champlain, the French explorer who founded Quebec in 1608 and laid the foundations of French Canada, in a common predicament for Europeans abroad: he is trying to assert his mastery over Canada with only

Don Bernardo de Vargas Machuca, author of the first manual of guerrilla warfare, pictured at the front of his book. In his left hand he holds his sword, in his right a pair of compasses poised over America. His motto reads: 'To the sword and the compass, more and more and more and more'.

a handful of helpers – in this case, with only two other musketeers! Nevertheless, he succeeded because of his skill in dividing the Indians against each other. Hernan Cortes had conquered Mexico for Spain by the same method almost a century before. At the same time as Champlain was fighting the Indians in the far north of America, other Europeans were fighting other Indians in the deep south, in Chile. Since there were only a few hundred Europeans against tens of thousands of Indians, a special sort of warfare developed, known as the 'guerrilla' or 'little war'. Highly trained units of about thirty 'commandos' were sent off into the forest with enough food, including seeds to plant if necessary, and ammunition to last for two years. Under skilled leadership they drove back the Indians and gradually extended Spanish dominion further south. One of their leaders was called Bernardo de Vargas Machuca, and in 1599 when his fighting days were over he wrote a book about his experience of fighting in the forest. It is the first manual of guerrilla warfare ever written.

Vargas Machuca was an exception. Few old soldiers wrote sensibly about warfare. Indeed several of them could hardly write at all. Most of the numerous books about military training, arms and armour, strategy and tactics, were written by armchair theorists. In England alone some 624 military books were published between 1471 and 1642. The writers were normally politicians, men of leisure, even mathematicians. They were men who had great learning but little practical experience of the wars. But even they did not think of using pictures to express themselves: they tried to do it with words alone, and it was not easy. Try to describe, using words only, how to make three ranks of soldiers into a single line . . . and then read the description on the next page by the sixteenth-century English military theorist, Sir John Smythe.

Ideas improved in the seventeenth century. Books were published in increasing numbers which did the obvious thing and printed a series of pictures to illustrate the various stages in

These two pages of description (and more follows in the original) are concerned with the simple problem of how to make three ranks of soldiers into a single line.

be of equall frunt & in equall distances with the said ranks before them. And further, if the captain of the same band his cōpany marching in their simple & single order of 5. in a rank as they did at ye first be disposed to haue two rāks to enter into one, that is whereas they marched before 5. in a ranke to make them 15. then hee is to say to the Sergeants of his band: *Triple your rankes by right line*, which briefe words by the Captain being pronounced, then the Sergeants presentlie are to command the drommers to strike the tripling of the rankes, or else themselues with the like briefe speeches as aforesaid, to cause the second and third ranks of any weapon to enter into the first ranke of the same weapon, and the fift and the sixt, to enter into the fourth, and the eigth and the ninth to enter into the seuenth, and so subsequentlie all the rest of the rankes orderly to performe the like, which being by them performed, they must presentlie in euery ranke inlarge themselues in their distances. And to the same effect, If a Captain be disposed to triple the rankes of the armed men of his band by flanks; that is, whereas they marched before but 5. in euery ranke in their single order, that he would reduce them into 15. in euery ranke, then he or his Lieutenant, or the Sergeants of his band may commaund the tripling of the ranks by saying to the first rankes. *Triple your ranks soldiors by both the flanks throughout.* Vppon which briefe speaches pronounced either by the Captain, Lieutenant, or Sergeants, the second & third ranks are presentlie to march vp to the flanks of the first ranke, that is to be vnderstood, that the second rank shall march to the right flanke of the first ranke, and the third ranke to the left flanke of the said first ranke, vntill they be al of one equall frunt, and in like and equall distances; at which time likewise the fift and sixt ranks shall in the very same order and sort march vp to both the flankes of the fourth ranke, and the eighth and the ninth ranks shall march vp to both the flanks of the seuenth rank, and so subsequentlie all the rest of the ranks that are of any one sort of weapon
pon

How Captains should triple their rankes by flanks.

It is to be noted that in all reducements of squadrons into forme with the compertiments of bands, that the middlemost part of the frunte is the highest place in estimation, and that the right hand of the same frunt is the second in degree, and that the left

pon shall march vp to both the flanks of the ranks of the like sort of weapon before them: so as of 5. that euerie rank did at the first consist in their simple and single order they are now by this trypling of rankes by both the flanks as aforesaid reduced, to be .15. in euerie ranke throughout. But because by this kinde of trypling of rankes, as also in trypling of them by right lyne, the fourth ranke is now become to be the second ranke, and the seuenth the third rank, and so subsequently in the rest, and that therfore euery one of those rankes are too great a distance by flanke the one from the other, they must euerie ranke presently vpon their first trypling performed, march vp vntill they finde themselues in such conuenient distances and nearenes by flankes one ranke to another, as the Captaine, Lieutenant or Seargeants shal thinke requisite.

But here it is to be noted that in case the last ranke or the two last rankes shall by this kinde of trypling and reducing by flankes as aforesaid, lacke a third ranke before them to reduce themselues vnto, by flanks, then the formost of the two last rankes shall marche vp by the right flanke of the piquers, vntill they come to the middle place whereas the Ensignebearer with his Ensigne doth stand, and there shall ranke and place themselues on the right hand of the Ensignebearer. At which present time likewise, the last ranke of the other .5. piquers shall march vp by the leste flanke of the armed men vntill they come to the foresaid midle place where the Ensignebearer with his Ensigne doth stand, and there shall ranke and place themselues on the left flanke of the Ensignebearer. And this is to be performed, by reason that it is not sufferable according to discipline that any broken ranke of a squadron of piquers, or of any other weapon of disequall nomber to the rest of the rankes should so march either in frunt or backe. Howbeit the Captaine before he commandeth the trypling of the rankes as aforesaid, ought well to consider of the nomber of the rankes

hand of the same frunt is the lowest place in degree. And that the first, second and thirde rankes, but chiefly the first, are the places of greatest estimation for the gentlemen of the bands if there be any to bee placed in the presence of their Captains to shewe their valours.

How & where any ouerplus of broken rankes of piquers should place themselues.

It is contrary to discipline that any ranke of disequall number to the rest of the rankes should march either in frunt or backe.

each military manoeuvre. In this book there are several pictures taken from three of the earliest (and best) works of this kind: on pages 12–13 and 35 Jacob de Gheyn, *The Use of Weapons: Arquebus, Musket and Pike* (first published in Holland in 1607); pages 15 and 19 Johan Jakob von Wallhausen, *Military Prowess on Horseback*; pages 16 and 49 *Military Prowess on Foot* (published in Germany in 1616). On this page is a picture from one of the best military manuals of the seventeenth century, a Dutch book by Jan Boxel published in 1673, showing exactly how musketeers should be trained to fire a 'salvo', each rank coming forward, firing, and then going to the back to reload their guns while the others fired.

These illustrated books were useful, but they were no good on their own. Many an inexperienced captain found to his horror as he drilled his men that he had forgotten the correct word of command and had to shout: 'Hold! Stand still until I have looked in my book!'

If raw officers were often unfamiliar with the orders necessary to drill their men, the soldiers themselves were normally little better. In Elizabethan England there were just four days in the year when all able-bodied men had to turn out and be trained to handle weapons, to march, and to recognize the basic words of command. Only Spain did better than this. Since the king of Spain also ruled over much of Italy, the Netherlands and central and southern America, it became normal to send new recruits for the army to serve in a garrison in a peaceful area for their first few months, so that they could learn drill, discipline and weapon-handling in safety. When they were properly trained they were sent off to an army on active service and more new recruits arrived to take their place. This system worked extremely well but, as far as we know, it was only used by Spain. Perhaps this helps to explain why Spanish troops in the sixteenth century were so much better than any others.

Despite the failure of most governments to provide any basic

The 'countermarch' was devised by the commanders of the Dutch army in 1594, and it was intended to provide a barrage of continuous fire from a formation of musketeers. Each man fired, and then went to the rear in order while the ranks behind him fired in turn. As the musket's design was improved, it became possible to speed up the operation: the earliest version of the manoeuvre involved ten ranks, because it took a long time to reload after firing. In this diagram by Jan Boxel, published in 1673, there are only four ranks.

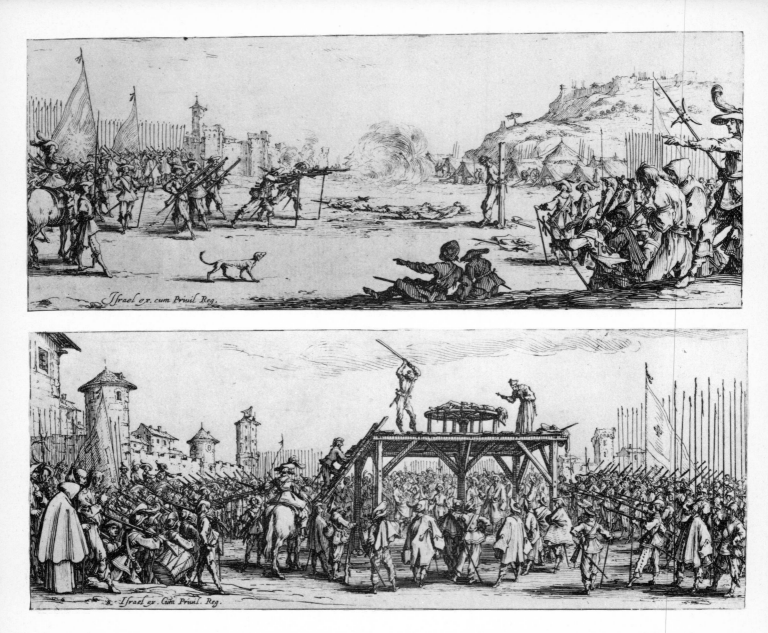

These two engravings, published in The Miseries of War by Jacques Callot in 1633, show military justice in action. Soldiers are being punished, some by simple execution, others by torture, for misbehaving. Callot, who was born in Lorraine and lived there during the wars of the mid-seventeenth century, probably based his chillingly realistic pictures on first-hand experience.

training for their troops, soldiers were expected to behave themselves with great restraint. There was a complicated code of behaviour, called the 'Articles of War', which laid down in great detail what they could and could not do. Failure to obey the 'Articles' brought heavy penalties. Many offences, even the theft of goods worth more than one shilling, were punished by death. Some were punished by death with torture. Other offences brought whippings, beatings, fines or extra duties.

Here are two pictures by a famous artist who lived while the Thirty Years War was being fought and drew what he saw. In both cases the punishments are carried out in front of all the troops in order to show everyone in the army what happened to those who misbehaved. Perhaps the soldiers in the first picture had fallen asleep on duty or had tried to desert. Perhaps those in the second picture had done something more serious like trying to incite a mutiny or, the worst offence a soldier could commit, betraying the password of the army to the enemy. That was treason.

3 Active service

During the whole of the century covered by this book there was only *one* year in which no war was being fought between various European states: 1610. And even in that year great armies were on the move and a major war was only just averted. Several states were at war for almost half the period and one, Spain, was at war for almost the whole of it. Few wars were straightforward duels between two countries; most were prolonged struggles involving several groups of allies. War was as much the normal state of Europe as peace. The series of maps opposite illustrate where the principal wars were fought.

The campaign of 1634

On 23 June 1634 an army of 19,000 Spanish troops left Milan in Italy to cross the Alps into Germany. They were led by the king of Spain's brother, Prince Ferdinand, and they had two aims. The first was to search out and destroy an army of Swedish troops in southern Germany; the second was to defeat the Dutch 'rebels' in the Netherlands. Spain was fighting two wars at the same time. There was the Thirty Years War in Germany (1618–1648), in which the German Protestants, helped by Sweden, France, England and Scotland, were trying to defeat the German Catholics, helped by Spain. Then there was the Eighty Years War in the Netherlands (1568–1648), in which the Dutch, helped again from time to time by France and England, were trying to become independent of Spain.

The fate of both wars seemed to depend on the success of Prince Ferdinand's expedition. If he could defeat the German Protestants and their allies, and if he could defeat the Dutch, Spain would remain the strongest power in Europe; if Ferdinand were defeated, Spain would have to make peace.

Luckily for us, there were three people in Ferdinand's army who kept a journal of what happened to them on the campaign. There was the prince's secretary, who kept an official logbook of all the orders issued to the troops; there was a friend of the

The Cardinal-Prince, Don Ferdinand, brother of Philip IV of Spain; born in 1609, died in 1641; Spanish governor of Catalonia 1632-3, of Lombardy 1633-4, and of the Netherlands 1634-41. He is shown here in a painting of the battle of Nördlingen, by Rubens.

Wars in Europe 1550–1650

0   500 miles
0   1000 km

Areas at war

1550-9 War between the Habsburgs and their enemies – led by France and the Turks – lasts almost the whole decade. Ivan the Terrible conquers part of the Volga valley from the allies of the Turks.

1560-9 Great Northern War between the Baltic powers, 1563-70. Rebellion in Scotland, France and the Netherlands. Turkish attacks in Hungary and the Mediterranean.

1570-9 Rebellion in Ireland and the Netherlands. Civil war in France. War in the eastern Baltic lands and on the Mediterranean.

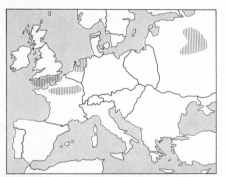

1580-9 War in France and the Netherlands continues. Spain and England at war (Spanish Armada, 1588). Rebellions in Russia.

1590-9 War between France, England and the Dutch, on one side, and Spain on the other. New wars in the Baltic and in Hungary.

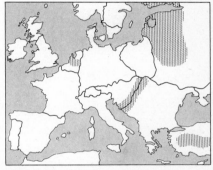

1600-9 The Dutch revolt continues, as does fighting in the Baltic and the war in Hungary. Rebellions in the Ottoman Empire.

1610-19 The 'Time of Troubles' in the Baltic continues, but elsewhere there is peace.

1620-9 War begins again in the Netherlands and continues in the Baltic. The Thirty Years War spreads through the Holy Roman Empire.

1630-9 The Thirty Years War continues, with France engaged against the Habsburgs after 1635.

1640-9 The Thirty Years War continues until 1648, as does the war in the Netherlands. Civil wars and rebellions break out in England, the Ukraine, Naples and Sicily. The Turks attack Venetian Crete.

far left: *Estebanillo Gonzalez, 'buffoon, author and composer' of a most entertaining account of Prince Ferdinand's march to the Netherlands in 1634. This portrait was printed in the book, but 'Gonzalez' was almost certainly a false name, and up to the present no one is quite sure who the real author of* The Life and Deeds of Estebanillo Gonzalez *might have been.*

left: *A seventeenth-century satire on the soldier, from Ireland. Even the shoe-buckles are made of food.*

right: *Pitching camp, from Wallhausen's* Military Prowess on Foot.

prince who noted down all that happened in a diary; and there was a soldier-cook, Estebanillo Gonzalez, who wrote down and later published an account of his exploits on the way to the Netherlands. His 'memoirs' have been translated into English eight times.

The prince's men were ready for the march in the spring of 1634, but they had to wait until June for the Alpine passes to clear of snow. Meanwhile they were trained, drilled and given new equipment in preparation for their long journey. However, not all the soldiers were properly equipped. Estebanillo Gonzalez remembered that his musket was tied together with string because its hammer and stock were broken, and he therefore filled his powder flasks with pepper and salt so that, as he put it, 'he could eat properly even if he could not fight'. For the same reason he substituted for his military sword three kitchen knives, one large, one small, and one medium-sized, in order to deal effectively with every sort of food which might come his way. In the end he must have looked like the English

soldier caricatured in the seventeenth-century drawing above who carried all his meals *and* his kitchen around with him!

Even so, Estebanillo could not avoid marching. He had to keep up with his fellow-soldiers as they marched through the Alps to Munich in Bavaria, where they would be joined by an army of German Catholics. Unfortunately for them, in June and July the Alpine valleys were still full of melting snow and the army's progress was very slow. First the road was blocked by an avalanche; then some troops were stranded when a river flooded. Before long, food began to run short and in the cold mountain nights the soldiers began to suffer from exposure. (The Stelvio pass, which the army had to cross, was over 9,000 feet, or 2,750 m high.) It was only after three gruelling weeks in the high passes that the army reached Innsbruck on the other side of the Alps. There the troops rested and were paid. Those in need were given warmer clothes and new boots; those who had misbehaved or tried to desert on the journey were punished.

After a long rest at Innsbruck, the army reached Munich on 24 August. They were now relatively close both to the forces of the German Catholics, their allies, and to the Swedish and German Protestants, their enemies. Advancing very cautiously on 2 September they came to the outskirts of Nördlingen, a town north-west of Munich, and there they joined forces with the German Catholic army. The troops made camp that night very carefully indeed. This illustration from a military textbook of the time shows how it was done. The baggage-waggons (which are numerous) are drawn into a semi-circle based on the river. The musketeers stand guard behind it while forage parties bring in sheep, cows and pigs (some even by boat) to feed the troops, and hay to feed the horses. The field kitchens, at each end of the first three rows in the camp, have smoke rising as they begin to cook the evening meal. It would have warmed the heart of Estebanillo Gonzalez.

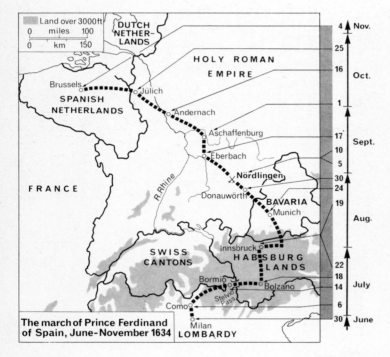

Land over 3000ft
miles 100
km 150

DUTCH NETHER-LANDS

HOLY ROMAN EMPIRE

Brussels
Jülich
SPANISH NETHERLANDS
Andernach
Aschaffenburg
Eberbach
Nördlingen
FRANCE
R. Rhine
Donauwörth
BAVARIA
Munich
SWISS CANTONS
Innsbruck
HABSBURG LANDS
Bormio
Bolzano
Stelvio Pass
Como
Milan
LOMBARDY

4 Nov.
25
16 Oct.
1
17 Sept.
10
5
30
24
19 Aug.
22
18
14 July
6
30 June

The march of Prince Ferdinand of Spain, June–November 1634

The battle of Nördlingen

Elaborate precautions around the camp were necessary for Prince Ferdinand's army because the main Protestant force, numbering about 25,000 men, was not far away. On the night of 5–6 September it advanced stealthily with the intention of making a surprise attack on Prince Ferdinand's sleeping soldiers. But the advance was led by some wagons and heavy cannon and these got stuck in the mud and, in the dark, some hit trees and boulders and overturned with a resounding crash. The Spanish troops were roused and the Protestants could advance no further until dawn. Then the battle began in earnest.

Prince Ferdinand's troops, some 33,000 men, were drawn up in a line between Nördlingen and a steep hill known as the Altbuch, about 1,500 feet (457 metres) high. The Protestants decided to make their principal attack on this hill, even though it was defended by the crack Spanish infantry.

The first charge was a resounding success: Prince Ferdinand's troops were shaken and began to fall back. It began to look like a great Protestant victory . . . but seventeenth-century battles were seldom so simple. As the Protestants advanced, two of their regiments mistook each other for the enemy and started fighting all over again. With only scarves and coloured plumes showing it was hard to distinguish friend from foe at a distance, especially through the smoke made by the muskets. As they fought, fire caught a powder store left behind by the retreating Catholics and it blew up among the advancing Protestants with a devastating explosion. Hundreds were thrown into the air and killed.

Seeing his chance, Prince Ferdinand ordered a cavalry charge before the Protestants had time to recover from their confusion. Gaining speed from their downhill run, the great horses, each one carrying a rider with a flashing broadsword, were soon dealing out death to their enemies. But here again the tide turned. The Swedish regiments were tough and experienced too, and they managed to rally and check the Spanish onslaught. Before long they were advancing again.

This time, the Spaniards formed squares and stood their ground. Every time the advancing Swedes took aim and fired, the Spaniards dropped to their knees so that the bullets went over their heads. Then they fired and many Swedes dropped down – dead. Those who managed to reach the infantry squares were impaled on the pikes of the Spaniards.

The Protestants charged fifteen times in the hope of breaking the Spanish squares; but the seven hours of carnage brought them no success. At last they recognized that all further efforts would be in vain and they prepared to retreat.

Hans Holbein's early sixteenth-century engraving captures the chaos and danger of hand-to-hand fighting in all periods. The pikemen at Nördlingen must have been locked in battle in much the same way.

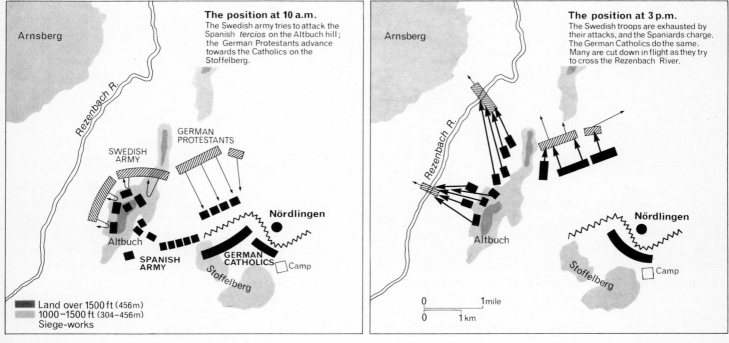

The position at 10 a.m.
The Swedish army tries to attack the Spanish *tercios* on the Altbuch hill; the German Protestants advance towards the Catholics on the Stoffelberg.

Arnsberg

Rezenbach R.

SWEDISH ARMY

GERMAN PROTESTANTS

Nördlingen

Altbuch

SPANISH ARMY

GERMAN CATHOLICS

Stoffelberg

Camp

■ Land over 1500 ft (456m)
▨ 1000–1500 ft (304–456m)
Siege-works

The position at 3 p.m.
The Swedish troops are exhausted by their attacks, and the Spaniards charge. The German Catholics do the same. Many are cut down in flight as they try to cross the Rezenbach River.

Arnsberg

Rezenbach R.

Altbuch

Nördlingen

Stoffelberg

Camp

0   1 mile
0   1 km

This bird's eye view of the battle was printed shortly after it actually took place. It shows a slightly later stage in the fighting than the similar view of the battle of Naseby on pages 36-7. Here we see the Swedish troops falling back as the Spaniards (in the foreground) advance on the left wing. The Catholic cavalry charges home on the right and in the distance the first Protestant riders have crossed the Rezenbach and are galloping to safety. In the right fore-

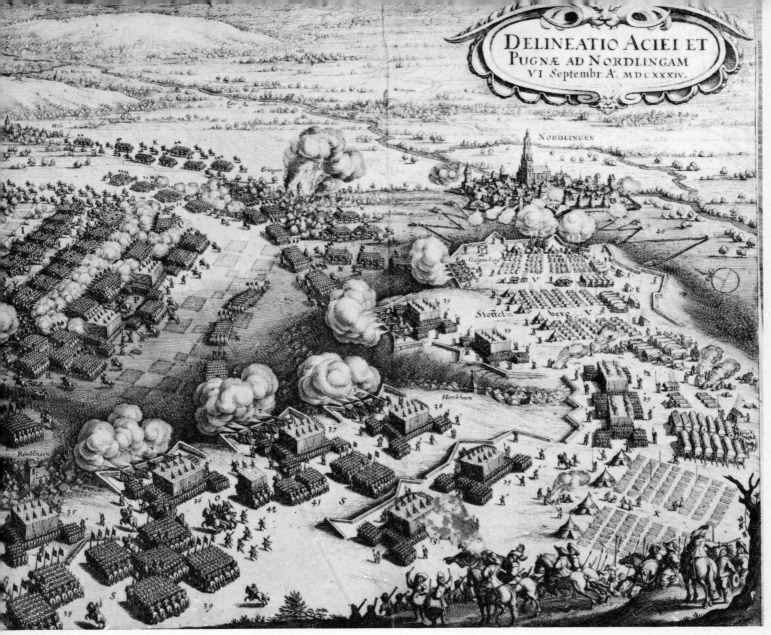

ground we can see the Catholic camp on the Stoffelburg, with the women and camp-followers going about their business through the heat of the fighting. After the victory, the troops will still need to be fed. It was no doubt here, among the women and the camp-fires, that Estebanillo Gonzalez hid himself until the battle had been won.

53

The Swedes on the right flank fell back and began to retire across the Rezenbach, a tributary of the Danube. This presented Prince Ferdinand with a golden opportunity: seeing the Swedes crossing the stream in some disorder, he commanded his whole line to advance. A great cry went up: *Santiago!* (St James!) *Cierra España!* (Get 'em Spain!), and the Spaniards surged forward for the kill. On the other flank, by Nördlingen, the German Catholic army, which had been holding its ground all day against the German Protestants, also charged forward. The Protestants were tired, dazed and disordered. Some of them were cut down where they stood; others were killed as they fled. Perhaps 6,000 men were left dead on the field, and about 6,000 more were captured, including the Swedish commander-in-chief, Gustav Horn.

Of course the Spaniards had suffered losses too. Many men had died during the first Protestant attack, and the constant bombardment by field artillery and small arms fire accounted for many more, including a captain standing right at Prince Ferdinand's side as he directed operations. Estebanillo Gonzalez, however, survived unscathed. The noise of the opening salvos had been too much for him: he could stand no more. So he jumped into a hole in the ground next to a dead horse and pretended to be its dead rider. He only ventured out when he heard the Spaniards shouting 'Victory, victory' and saw for himself the Protestants in flight with his comrades in hot pursuit. Then he leapt to his feet, drew his largest kitchen knife and joined in the chase to 'slice up some Swedes', stabbing and stealing from the dead and dying left on the field and plundering their belongings, just like the callous soldiers in the picture on the cover.

The results of the battle

For five days after the battle, Estebanillo and his fellow Spaniards feasted on the meat, bread and wine which the

Plundering soldiers must have looked like this at almost all times. This picture was published in 1573, but burning, looting and wanton destruction were as common in the wars of the mid-seventeenth century as in those of the mid-sixteenth.

Protestants had left behind in their flight. Rewards were given to the soldiers who had shown particular courage or skill in the victory. Many of the German Protestants taken prisoner at Nördlingen, as in other battles, changed sides and fought their next campaign along-side their former enemies. Then on 10 September Prince Ferdinand formed his men into a single column and began to march north again to the Netherlands. Brussels was still over 300 miles (480 km) away, the roads were poor and the countryside, according to Prince Ferdinand's diarist, was like a desert: the villages burned to the ground, the fields uncultivated, the few surviving inhabitants reduced to starving shadows. The army did not reach their goal until

4 November 1634, just two months after the victory at Nördlingen, and four months since they had left Italy.

Nördlingen was indisputably a great victory, one of the most glorious ever won by Spanish troops, but it brought Spain few lasting benefits. A famous French writer of the sixteenth century, Michel de Montaigne, once observed that 'It isn't a victory unless it wins the war'. Nördlingen proved how true that was. Although after the battle much of southern Germany fell into the hands of the German Catholics, and although Prince Ferdinand arrived in the Netherlands with a reputation for military success, the total defeat of the German Protestants thoroughly alarmed France.

As the map shows, France in the early seventeenth century was encircled by Spain, Spanish Italy, Spanish Burgundy and the Spanish Netherlands. Now there was the prospect of a Spanish Germany as well. That was the last thing that France wished to see. The French government began to fear that unless war was declared on Spain at once, Prince Ferdinand's victorious troops, fresh from their success in Germany, would reconquer the rebellious Netherlands and then turn on France. As one Spanish statesman described the encirclement, 'The heart of the Spanish Empire is France'. It was in order to prevent this threat becoming fact that in May 1635 France declared war on Spain and sent armies into the Spanish Netherlands to engage the troops of Prince Ferdinand. Instead of defeating the Dutch, the prince now found he had to defend himself against France.

After thirteen more years of fighting in the Netherlands and Germany, Spain agreed to peace, although the war with France dragged on until 1659. Spain could not afford the expense of war on three fronts any longer: the cost of her troops was too great. This was good news for almost everyone in Spain (wars are seldom popular with taxpayers) but it was bad news for the soldiers themselves. For many of them, the army was the only way of life they knew. What would they do, what could they do, when they left the ranks?

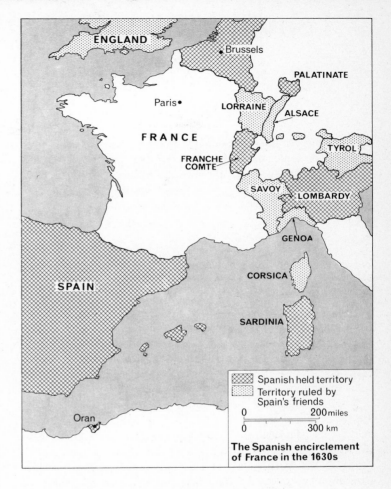

Spanish held territory
Territory ruled by Spain's friends

0   200 miles
0   300 km

The Spanish encirclement of France in the 1630s

4 Leaving the army

Every army on active service lost many of its men each year. Some died, some were injured or fell sick, and others simply deserted. Taken together, these causes reduced the strength of even the best units in an army by at least a fifth, and some units might lose three-quarters of their men in a year.

Desertion

No army allowed its soldiers any leave or holidays. Once a man joined up, he was expected to serve without a break until either the war came to an end or he did. Even the peasant had many 'holy days' in the year, that is, days on which his church did not allow him to work; not so the soldier. Some wars went on for years, some for a lifetime, and there were no 'days off'. Soldiers might have to fight even at Christmas. Add this to the hardships and dangers and it is not surprising that many soldiers tried to escape. They deserted.

Some of the deserters were young soldiers who felt homesick. Others resented the harsh discipline or wretched conditions. Some were simply afraid. Certainly desertion was highest when the fighting was heaviest. At the Spanish siege of Bergen-op-Zoom in the Netherlands in 1622, for example, the besiegers had 20,600 men in July, but only 13,200 in October. Many of the deserters were so desperate that they even fled to the town they were besieging! Some people of the town who wrote a journal of the siege, noted: 'From dawn until dusk one could see the soldiers jumping like rabbits from their holes, leaving the trenches, hedges, thickets and ditches where they had hidden in order to run breathless to the town.'

Those who reached Bergen complained bitterly of their treatment in the trenches, of how their officers drove them on with blows 'like sheep to the slaughter', of how they served without pay. In Bergen they pleaded pitiably for 'A little bread and a little money' and, of course, for a passage home. Many other soldiers of the besieging army made their escape by some

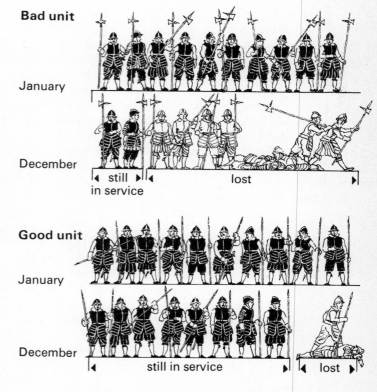

Bad unit

January

December

◄ still ►◄   lost   ►
in service

Good unit

January

December

◄   still in service   ►◄ lost ►

other route. From the walls of Bergen the guards regularly saw Spanish sentries slyly leave their posts, pretending to cut grain, hay or wood, or to search for vegetables to dig up. They strayed further and further from the camp, finally making their break for freedom. One day towards the end of the siege, a deserter from the Spanish camp staggered up to the town walls.

'Where have you come from?' asked the watch.

'From Hell', he replied.

Amputation, with a bucket underneath to catch the blood. The patient looks unconscious; either he has fainted with the pain, or he is dead drunk, or perhaps the cloth over his face is soaked with the juice of some plant which has drugged him. This woodcut, like the one on page 58, is from a manual of military surgery by Hans von Gersdorff, 1517; the first ever published.

Wounds

Naturally, being a soldier was a dangerous occupation. Many were killed outright; many more were badly wounded and remained deformed or crippled for life, unable to earn a living any more.

In the sixteenth and seventeenth centuries nobody really knew how the human body worked. People often recovered from their illnesses and injuries in spite of, rather than because of, any treatment or medicines they received.

However, the soldier wounded in action was often more fortunate than the peasant who fell off a haystack or under a horse: army doctors and surgeons were the best available. Mending broken bodies each and every day was their trade, and, not surprisingly, they became very good at it. Many of them developed new techniques, and the woodcut shows one of them. The patient has something wrong with his right leg – perhaps a badly broken bone or a crushed foot. In those days the only solution was to cut off, or 'amputate', the damaged limb. This could be done quite quickly: one cut and three strokes with a saw would be enough. The other pictures show the instruments used. The problem was to stop the bleeding

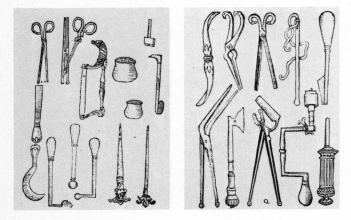

left: *A selection of the ornate instruments used by the experienced military surgeon of the sixteenth century: saws, knives, axes, pliers, even a brace and bit . . . Not for nothing were surgeons popularly referred to as 'saw-bones'.*

and prevent infection. Most doctors believed that the only solution was to burn, or 'cauterize', all the flesh around the amputation, even though this was agonizingly painful for the patient. In the sixteenth century, however, it was found that if the wound was painted with thick animal fat it healed just as well and much less painfully. But it still hurt.

Sometimes doctors had to operate on the field of battle itself. The woodcut here shows a soldier who has something in his chest, not far from his heart. The doctor tries to cut the missile out while his assistant (who is armed in case the enemy's troops break through) holds the patient from behind. The soldier is gripping his chair and putting on a brave face, but there are no anaesthetics. The doctor is doing his best, but his scalpel has not been sterilized and neither he nor his assistants are wearing gloves or masks. Probably they have not even bothered to wash their hands! No one knew about germs in the sixteenth century and, even if an operation like this was successful, the patient would often die later because his wound became infected.

What happened to those who lost arms and legs? If they were lucky they might be given a post in some peaceful garrison town as a watchman, or they might be given a small government pension. In many cases, however, they would be left with no other alternative than to beg for a living. Only the very favoured were given an artificial limb, although it was perfectly possible to make them as you can see opposite.

There were very few permanent military hospitals in Europe during the sixteenth and seventeenth centuries. In fact only Spain tried to care properly for her wounded soldiers. Every army of the king of Spain was provided with a complete military hospital, staffed by trained doctors and surgeons. The Spanish army in the Netherlands, which fought continually from 1572 until 1659, was served by a hospital at Mechelen (in what is now Belgium) which had 330 beds and a staff of between sixty and a hundred people (from the chief

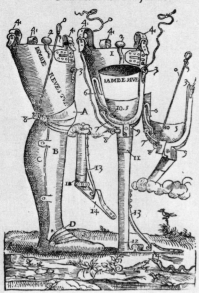

Pourtraict des iambes artificielles.

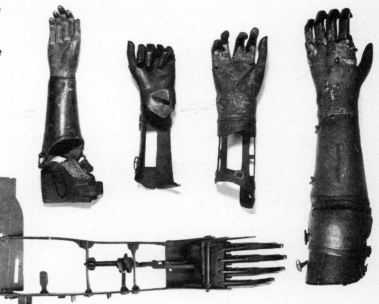

Artificial limbs available to wounded soldiers in the sixteenth century. On the left we see some models of false legs designed by the foremost military doctor of the later sixteenth century, Ambroise Paré. On the right are some actual artificial arms designed for patients in the sixteenth century.

doctor down to the women who did the laundry). This was also one of the very few 'teaching hospitals' in Europe, where the doctors had pupils with them to learn how to carry out operations. Other smaller mobile hospitals accompanied the Spanish army on its campaigns.

All Spanish soldiers received their hospital treatment free. Every month they had a basic wage of 30 *reales* but 1 *real* of this was kept back to be put towards the cost of running the hospital. Actually the hospital cost about three times as much as the total of what everybody had contributed, and so the government had to pay the rest itself.

This was a surprisingly modern system, but it was unique. No other country cared for its wounded soldiers as well as Spain did. Queen Elizabeth I, for instance, had a different way with her troops. After the defeat of the Spanish Armada in 1588, she refused all requests to provide any money for the heroes who had fought the Spanish fleet. Those who were injured in the action were left to starve to death, crippled and spent, in the Channel ports. Wounded English veterans only began to receive disability pensions in 1593 when an Act of Parliament declared: 'It is agreeable with Christian charity, policy, and the honour of our nation that such as have since

the 25th day of March 1588 adventured their lives and lost their limbs or disabled their bodies, or shall hereafter adventure their lives, lose their limbs or disable their bodies in the defence and service of her majesty and the state, should at their return be relieved and rewarded to the end [that] they may reap the fruit of their good deserving, and others may be encouraged to perform the like endeavours.' It was, indeed, very 'agreeable' with charity, policy and national honour, but perhaps it should have been done in 1588!

Diseases

Of course, the army's doctors had other things besides injuries to deal with. Soldiers were as likely as civilians to fall victims to many deadly germs, for most of which there was then no cure: plague, smallpox, dysentery, malaria, tuberculosis . . . In many ways the soldiers were *more* likely to catch these diseases than civilians, because infection spreads more easily in crowded conditions, especially where people are underfed or badly fed, as they were in the army. Dysentery, for example, was also called 'camp fever' because so many soldiers' camps were ravaged by it.

There was one disease which was especially common among soldiers: syphilis. At any one time perhaps one quarter of all the soldiers in the Spanish army in the Netherlands had syphilis. The disease was so common that the government paid the military hospital at Mechelen a special grant every year to treat all affected soldiers. It was no doubt the same in other armies. Certainly in the sixteenth and seventeenth centuries syphilis was far more dangerous than it is today, and there was no cure. The infected soldiers broke out in sores and after some years of terrible pain and disfigurement they went mad and died. Until this happened, all the doctors could do was to give the victims steam baths and mercury ointments, cauterize the sores, and send them back to active service.

Death

In the Middle Ages, many European soldiers prided themselves on the chivalrous respect they showed towards their enemies. They took care, whenever possible, not to kill their enemy (or his horse). Instead they tried to take him prisoner and, later, to sell him for ransom. In our period, however, all too often soldiers and civilians were killed indiscriminately when they fell into the hands of their enemies. The picture on page 4 shows what could happen: the soldiers in the foreground are disarmed and defenceless, but they are still going to have their throats cut. This scene was painted in 1616 by Sebastian Vrancx of Antwerp, and it was meant to refer to the conduct of soldiers during the war between Spain and the Dutch Republic. The print of Haarlem, from the 1570s, is of the same conflict and, although it is meant to be propaganda, emphasizing the brutality of the Spanish troops, it relates to a real event: the treacherous execution of a number of Dutch burghers. In the early stages of the Dutch Revolt, and also at times during the German Thirty Years War, both sides regularly killed all their prisoners.

HAERLEM.

For normal circumstances, however, when a soldier was fatally wounded or weakened by disease, there was a chaplain attached to every company, at least in theory, to help dying men to prepare for the life which, according to the teaching of the Christian churches, would follow death. The chaplains provided church services and religious instruction for the men in their charge, and their families. They preached every week and carried out the necessary marriages, baptisms and burials. Some of these chaplains were good men with genuine religious

On 13 July 1573 the town of Haarlem in Holland surrendered to the Spanish army, which had been besieging it since the end of 1572. It surrendered in return for a promise that none of the defenders would be harmed. However, as soon as they were in control, the Spaniards hanged a number of burghers and beheaded many of the garrison for their resistance. Others were tied back-to-back and thrown into the river. This print, issued in Germany at the time, was intended to whip up anti-Spanish feeling.

The helmet and sword of the Zurich reformer, Huldreych Zwingli, killed at the battle of Cappel in 1531.

convictions, men like the zealous Puritan, Hugh Peter, in Cromwell's army during the English Civil War, or the Swiss reformer, Huldreych Zwingli, who served as a military chaplain until he died in battle at the head of his men. But not all chaplains were as fearless and devout as Zwingli. From the Spanish army there are reports of chaplains who traded in forged saints' heads (as a side-line) and of chaplains who exploited the fact that most of the soldiers in their charge could not write. Since the men could not write, they could not make a will. On their death-beds, therefore, when they begged the chaplain to make a will for them, many unscrupulous chaplains refused to do so unless the soldier left a considerable legacy to them!

Probably the standard of most chaplains fell somewhere in between these two extremes. Life as an army padre was hard and dangerous, and the pay was poor. Most of them no doubt did their best to console their men, especially when they faced death in the service of their country, and of their religion.

Discharge

Of course, not all soldiers died or deserted or became cripples. There were some who survived until, eventually, the war came to an end. What happened to them?

The troops were mustered for the last time, their weapons were returned, and they received their arrears of wages in full. The troops were always paid in cash; normally the coins were dropped into each man's hat, just to make sure there was no mistake, and after that the men were free to go. Many of the veterans went home, back to wives, families and friends they had not seen for years; but after so many years of service many of them had no homes or relatives left to go to. Perhaps that is why many ex-soldiers soon went on to join up in another army fighting in another part of Europe. What else could they do? Being a soldier might be the only job they knew. Sometimes they even joined the very army they had been fighting against before!

This odd situation only changed in the seventeenth century. Until then it was most unusual for soldiers to be kept on in an army after peace was made. Most European governments could not afford a peacetime reserve force. As late as 1610 there were 'standing', or permanent, armies only in three parts of Europe: in the Netherlands, in the areas of Italy controlled by Spain (Sicily, Naples and Lombardy) and in Hungary (for defence against the Turks). Elsewhere there was just the royal bodyguard and a small garrison in a few strong-

points. In England the garrisons were at the Tower of London and at Berwick-upon-Tweed, Dover and a few other coastal towns. But things changed in the 1640s and 1650s. After the end of the German Thirty Years War, most of the German princes kept a considerable number of their soldiers as a permanent peacetime force and gradually moulded and trained them into a fighting elite. It was the same after the end of the war between Spain, the Dutch and the French: each of the warring powers kept back a part of its armed forces to form a permanent reserve. In England, when the civil wars ended in 1660, some of the best troops from both sides were formed into three separate regiments. The Coldstream Guards were recruited from among the Roundheads, the Grenadier Guards from among the Cavaliers, and the Life Guards from both. These regiments have continued to serve in the British army to this day.

The soldiers in these various new standing armies were very different from the soldiers we have been looking at in this book.

A regiment is disbanded in the main square of Utrecht, after a brief period of enlistment in 1618. The soldiers hand back their equipment to be stored in the special tent erected for the purpose, while the townspeople and soldiers from other regiments look on. Just as they began their military life by enlisting in the local inn, so they ended it in the main square. Barracks were a thing of the future.

They were all dressed and armed in the same way, as you can see overleaf. They all wore the same uniform. They spent their time drilling, training and practising the same movements all together. Government inspectors were sent out to make sure that they did it properly. The ordinary soldier was now a full-time professional, a regular. He had become an efficient cog in a permanent machine. The day of the modern soldier had dawned ... and you can find out about that in other books.

In 1751, almost exactly a century after the period covered in this book, David Morier painted a set of pictures to show the uniforms of all the regiments in the British army. During the 1740s there had been a series of regulations to make all regiments conform more closely to a standard. Here are grenadiers – men picked for their size and strength – of the first three regiments of foot:

the First, the Royal Scots;
the Second, the Queen's;
the Third, the Buffs.

Each regiment has its distinguishing marks: the upper badge on the grenadier cap, for example, or the lace on the coat, or colour of facings and turn-backs, or pattern of sword-hilt, or a combination of several of these details would mark out one regiment from its neighbours in the line of battle. The similarities, however, are much more obvious: the red coat, the cap badge of the white horse of Hanover, the standard equipment – Brown Bess musket, waist belt with small cartridge box, shoulder belt with large box behind and match-holder in front. All the men are standing in the same drill position. These are disciplined soldiers of a regular army.